FRONT ROW

ISBN: 9798344523347

Dedicated to Donna
My Proverbs 31 Partner
Always and Ever

FRONT ROW

Eight Grateful Decades

at the Political Parade

JOHN ANDREWS

TABLE OF CONTENTS

PROLOGUE
THE WEST STEPS

September 2023

Echoes of the Ghost Parade

The West Steps in better days, before the Civil War statue
was torn down in 2020 by a rogue element of the ghost parade

It was a perfect September day in 2023. The leaves were starting to turn; Denver was dressing herself for fall. The red Solara convertible turned right off Lincoln, then left off 14th Street, and stopped at the security gate on the south end of the State Capitol parking circle.

"Your name and your business here today, sir, please," said a woman's voice over the intercom.

"Former Senator John Andrews, here for an appointment with Governor Polis," the driver replied.

"Of course, Mr. President, good to see you today," came the answer as the gate arm went up. "Welcome back, sir. Lots of spaces today. Park anywhere, sir, and you take good care."

Driving slowly counterclockwise around the circle, Andrews felt a pleasant warmth. The flood of sunlight seemed a little more golden. *That's kind of nice. A few of them still remember, even after two decades.* What was two decades, though? His political memory now clocked in at eight decades. Eight decades and counting!

His years in the Colorado Senate, 1998–2005, the last two as presiding officer, had seemed like such a huge deal to John at the time. Now, not so much. Anybody could win a trivia contest by even remembering that era. *Who took the president's gavel from Stan Matsunaka and handed it on to Joan Fitz-Gerald; a nice-guy Republican sandwiched between two streetwise Democrats? Bonus question, double points.*

He found a space near the Capitol's grand main entry, the west steps, and got out, locking the car. Would it be safe here for half an hour? Probably yes, he thought; public building, broad daylight, after all. Yet downtown was deteriorating almost by the week, so who could say? Druggies and deranged street people, slouching everywhere, more of them all the time.

In his day there had been no vehicle security gates on the circle, no metal detectors at all the doors. Those dated from the national scare after 9/11. In his day there had been the statue of a Civil War soldier facing west, here on the brow of the hill, commemorating Colorado's role in helping save the Union and free the slaves. Its violent toppling and shamefaced removal dated from the endless summer of rioting in 2020.

Abolishing human bondage and reasserting constitutional government had for some reason become, as of then, no longer achievements but embarrassments in the American story. By what imaginable logic, what moral calculus? Andrews shook his head sadly. At least the Civil War street names still held, honoring Lincoln and three of his generals: Sherman, then Grant, then Logan.

Mount Blue Sky

Still held for now; but for how much longer? He squinted toward the western skyline, where Mount Evans—named for a great territorial governor and university founder (Northwestern, University of Denver)—was in process of being scrubbed from the history books and rechristened, pending permission from Indian tribes, as Mount Blue Sky. *Buckle up, boy. Cancel culture is coming for us all.*

His thoughts flashed back to a summer day in 1980 when he had climbed Mount Evans with his friend Monty Hoyt, son of the great *Denver Post* editor Palmer Hoyt. That had been the week a long-building spiritual crisis engulfed John, tearing away the moorings of his Christian Science upbringing and setting him on a new course to follow Jesus Christ.

In remembering it all now, his grim ruminations yielded to a surge of gratitude for all God's goodness to him—all the treasured memories he owed this old pile of granite with its marble halls and golden dome. It seemed the ghosts of politics past were walking with him, stride for stride, as he started up the west steps.

There was the formidable John Love, who had given Andrews for Governor a rocket boost with fellow Republicans. And the maverick Democrat Dick Lamm, whose quixotic provocations were just the foil Andrews needed in launching Colorado's first think tank.

There too was the charismatic, irrepressible Bill Armstrong, a young legislative phenom down here in the '60s who would become, by the '80s, a U.S. senator and presidential possibility. There were all the worldly-wise scribblers of the Capitol press corps in bygone days — Sanko and Blake of the *Rocky*, Brown and Ewegen of the *Post*, Hilliard of the AP, and so many more.

Atop the steps, finding the tall brass doors locked — one could still get out that way, but could no longer get in; security again — he muttered ruefully at his absentmindedness and turned to walk back down. Now, to his mind's eye, ghosts also thronged the nearby streets, Colfax over to his right, Lincoln straight ahead, a swirling spectral crowd evoking all the parades and rallies he'd seen here at Civic Center through the years.

Banners flying, they ranged from Veterans Day, Stock Show, and Cinco de Mayo to Martin Luther King Day and Christmas (er, holiday) lighting ceremonies. From demonstrations and protests to festivals and memorials to championships for all the home teams: Broncos, Nuggets, Rockies, Avalanche, what not.

The ethereal mingled sounds of cheers and chants, shouting and sirens, floated to him across the still autumn air. His ears rang with the swell of anthems, the tramp of marching bands, the roar of jet flyovers, the cacophony of horns honking, waves of thunderous applause,

And it occurred to John Andrews just then that his whole charmed and improbable life from 1944 to right now, eight grateful decades' worth, his love affair with America and its way of life, its form of government, its moment in world history, could all be summed up as a privileged observer's vantage point at exactly this kind of spectacle.

Doing Self-Government

Yes, that was it. He had had an unmatched front-row seat at a wonderful, breath-taking parade—the American political parade, a glorious procession of variety and striving and hope, an astonishing adventure of the human spirit, a free people "doing" self-government with all their hearts.

What had it all meant? Where was all of it leading? What could any one person do, other than marvel at the magnificence and madness of it all? *Well, you could write up what you saw at the parade. That would be doing something.*

So it would, he reflected. After all, his almost-eighty years spanned fully a third of America's history from the framing of the Constitution in 1787 to the troubled presidency of Joe Biden today. One spectator's account covering so long a duration ought to be worth compiling.

Nor had Andrews been strictly an observer the whole time. He'd had his moments as a participant. To make too much of those, though, would only be to embarrass himself with the grandiosity of a fly on a chariot wheel. *What a dust do I raise!* No, when the history of those decades came to be written, none of John's doings in the parade itself would warrant more than a footnote in 8-point type.

Thus was born the idea for this book, a bell that nothing could unring. The grand learning experience that had been his life in and around politics must be chronicled. His heart of thanks for these eight grateful decades must not go unexpressed.

He heard his name called from over by the Capitol's north doors. A burly figure with an infectious Irish grin was waving to him. It was former Speaker Frank McNulty, now a lobbyist for conservative causes; tough sledding in these Democrat-dominated times.

"Back again like a bad penny, I see," McNulty jibed.

"You know me, shrugged Andrews. "Can't resist returning to the scene of the crime."

Author's Note:

The foregoing scene is imaginary,
as is the scene in the epilogue (obviously).
Those are the only fictitious things in this book.
Everything else described here
really took place just as I have set it down.

CHAPTER ONE
FDR TO TRUMAN TO IKE

May 1944 – April 1954

A Stunning Upset

Repercussions from President Truman's dramatic victory
reached even sleepy little Fennville, Michigan

He would always remember the day Tom Dewey didn't beat Harry Truman. The Andrews boy was just four when that presidential election shocked the country, November 1948, and it would stand as his first historical memory for the next three quarters of a century.

Little Johnnie, or Bump as his father liked to call him, of course knew nothing as yet of Republicans and Democrats, liberals and conservatives, or what the 48 stars on the flag meant, or who lived in the White House and why it mattered. He knew only that *his* house was sunk in gloom because the wrong candidate, as far as his parents and grandparents were concerned, had won on Tuesday, and bad things might happen as a result.

None did, though, at least none dramatic enough to upend life in Fennville, the Michigan farming community where John's mother's father, business entrepreneur Marc Hutchinson, was the principal employer and a fervent Republican partisan. Another four years of Truman and his New Dealers was not what the country needed; of that Grandpa Hutchinson was sure. At least his son Edward, "Uncle Ender" to John, had won a second term in the Michigan legislature; Edward would go on to be a U.S. congressman in the 1960s and '70s.

This chronicle properly begins, however, back in May 1944 at the big white frame house on West Main in Fennville, snugly situated between the school on your right and the church on your left. John Kneeland Andrews, Jr., a pint-size newborn with a ten-gallon name, while as yet consciously cognizant of little else but bedtimes and mealtimes, was already taking in the pulsebeat of the American political parade with his mother's milk.

One of the boy's grandfathers had gone to West Point, the other to Annapolis. His father and uncles were among the 12 million Americans then in uniform as the United States and its allies bore down on Hitler's Germany and Tojo's Japan in the endgame of World War II. The Normandy invasion hadn't yet occurred, and President Franklin Roosevelt was still half a year from winning his fourth term. In the same month he did so, November 1944, U.S.S. *Archerfish*, the submarine on which John Sr. served, would earn a commendation from FDR for sinking the Japanese super-carrier *Shinano* off the mouth of Tokyo Bay.

Up the Pole

But even as the greatest armed conflict in human history built toward its climax, the infancy of the postwar world was stirring to life in its cradle close by that of baby Johnnie. The forces were gathering that would propel General Eisenhower like an arrow from the supreme command of D-Day to the presidency eight years later.

Future presidents Jack Kennedy, Lyndon Johnson, Richard Nixon, Gerald Ford, Jimmy Carter, Ronald Reagan, and George H. W. Bush would soon be out of uniform, launched in politics, and starting their climb up the greasy pole. The fabulously assertive Baby Boom generation, officially dating from 1946 (the year John's brother Jim was born) would soon favor us with Bill Clinton, George W. Bush, Donald Trump, and the last-born, Barack Obama; by which time Joe Biden (born 1942) was already far-famed as the mouthiest kid in Scranton, PA. Look out, world!

In policy as well as personalities, the postwar world was taking on sharper definition and direction as the boy grew. Wartime urgency abated after 1945, but global tensions hardly slackened. Winston Churchill, speaking at a college in Missouri in 1946, warned of an Iron Curtain being imposed across Europe by Stalin and the Soviets. America and its allies countered with NATO, the Marshall Plan, and the Berlin airlift.

Little John was oblivious to all of it, though China became a menacing reality to him in 1949 when Grandmother Hutchinson became terminally ill while visiting there, just before Mao and his Communist revolutionaries took power. June 1950 was seared on his memory with newspaper headlines on the outbreak of war in Korea, where MacArthur and his forces were soon in full retreat before the hordes of invading Chinese.

By then Marianne Andrews had given her sons two sisters, Eleanor and Sally, and John had started kindergarten in the Fennville public schools. John Sr. was finding time to serve on the school board, not because he had any political bent (he didn't) or because his father was a college professor, but because his father-in-law (and employer at Michigan Fruit Canners) thought it civically fitting and advantageous.

But a lifelong restless streak in John Sr. was already asserting itself, and he felt the need for more elbow room than what was afforded him as the fellow who had married the boss's daughter in a little factory town. By October 1950, Johnnie found himself a resident of St. Louis, Missouri, where his dad had grown up, and attending Principia, the Christian Science school his dad's parents had helped found.

So while the move had in one sense been a breakout for John Sr., a gesture of independence, in another sense he had simply moved from one family business to another. His restlessness was far from slaked, as time would soon tell. But John Jr., meanwhile, thrived on the change.

He and Jim, hankering to relive history, immersed themselves in Mark Twain's river lore, Jefferson's Louisiana Purchase, and the Lewis and Clark expedition. Grandfather Andrews took them to see Lincoln's New Salem. It thrilled the brothers to learn that their house had once belonged to the great Branch Rickey of Cardinals baseball renown. Living in border-state Missouri seemed to bring the Civil War era closer, and they convinced themselves (pure fancy though it was) that the house next door had once been a station on the Underground Railroad.

Black people, a rarity in western Michigan, filled whole neighborhoods here. To John they seemed forbidding yet fascinating, distinctly "other." His mother's colored cleaning lady, Ethel Bailey, had the warmest smile, the saddest eyes, and the most rollicking laugh of anyone he had ever known.

In those days of the early '50s, the boy lived with one foot in America's dynamic present and the other in its glorious past, transported there by his ever-growing shelf of Landmark Books, the Random House history series for young readers.

Come 1952 and another presidential election year, though, he still had no more profound concept of politics than the "good guys vs. bad guys" formula of a thousand TV westerns. Stevenson and the Democrats were the side we didn't like, we of the Andrews and Hutchinson families; Eisenhower and the Republicans were the side we liked. "I Like Ike" was how all the buttons and bumper stickers summed it up, in fact. What else did you need to know? Watching President Dwight D. Eisenhower and Vice President Richard Nixon be inaugurated on January 20, 1953, became John's first distinct memory of any news event on television.

Clubbable

No one would have predicted the youngster would someday run for office himself, or work as a broadcaster, or address crowds. Around other people, he was pleasant enough company, but serious-minded to a fault, and with a shyness that could seem like aloofness. Johnnie A, as he was now sometimes called, got tagged at school as "the brain" and often, I'm afraid, felt a subconscious sense of superiority. Truth be told, he'd probably rather that the A in his nickname should connote "admirable," more so than "amicable."

By working at it, however, he made himself—as the Brits would say—a reasonably clubbable fellow, forging relationships that would last for life. Pals who lived up the street, Principia classmates from age six, Jon Fisher, Rob Craig, and Karen Van Vleck, remain his treasured friends to this day. The Hutchinson cousins he and Jim summered with in 1951–54 at a lakeshore cottage near Fennville, Marc and Leland, became blood brothers to them forever. Though far from the gregarious extrovert his father was, thus did Johnnie A make his way.

Six weeks after Ike took office, March 1953, the news of Joseph Stalin's death came like a thunderclap. The boy had a vague sense that a page had turned; that an end was in sight from the constant unease of hot war and cold war that had hung over the first ten years of his life. Had it been, overall, a grateful decade?

Callow as he was, young Andrews knew enough to thank God for the high privilege of being an American.

Freedom and opportunity and affluence, liberty and justice
for all, flourished here as nowhere else on earth; of this he
never doubted.

Had America Peaked?

Much later, looking back in maturity, he would also be
grateful that his country had been generous and idealistic
enough, confident and determined enough, to retain the
mantle of world leadership after World War II and press forward, almost without missing a beat, in the Cold War struggle against godless communism. He would be grateful to live
under a Constitution strong enough to protect (for the most
part) dissenters in that struggle from unjust persecution.

And he would feel blessed as the joint heir of a vital
moral and spiritual tradition relentlessly pressing forward
toward equal rights for every human person regardless of
color. President Truman had desegregated the armed forces
in 1948. Chief Justice Warren would desegregate the schools
in 1954. A new day was coming, if belatedly.

Yet historians of the far future might have reason to look
back on that decade and conclude that what Henry Luce in
1941 had called the American Century was already peaking.
Of course Andrews couldn't have known it at the time, but
the indicators were there.

The U.S. nuclear monopoly was gone, stolen by Soviet
spies. China was lost to the Communists. Korea would
become the first in an unbroken string of no-win wars from
that day to this. Marxist penetration of American institutions,
briefly exposed in the Hiss case, sank from view after Senator
McCarthy imploded, but persisted as a silent malignancy in
the body politic — again, from that day to this.

Governance by We the People had already begun giving way to the dictates of judges and bureaucrats. America's role in the world over the next seven decades would come to seem less and less like leading, more and more like coping.

Right now, though, to the boy's wide eyes and crackling imagination, the American political parade was a glorious thing to behold—and maybe, indeed, some day to dabble in—albeit not all the marchers were quite in step, not all the trumpets in perfect tune.

VITAL SIGNS, 1950

The eighty-year span covered in this book works out to three or four generations. That's enough time for big changes to occur, compounding in such small increments that most people don't even notice. We're all busy with our own existence. Life, it's been said, is what happens while you're making other plans. And thus does the drowsy frog get boiled — or wake up to its peril and scramble to safety.

From boyhood, John Andrews was more inclined to think about ideas than data. But for that very reason, when it came to taking stock of eight grateful decades, he was curious to see what might be learned by charting some of America's vital signs at ten-year intervals across that period.

While the politically-minded were parading or watching the parade these eighty years, had the whole body politic been holding its own? Americans were obviously living more affluently — and longer. But were their habits, as a people, more those of Aesop's ant or his grasshopper: habits of prudence or of profligacy? Did they know better than to eat their seed corn?

Baseline data from 1950 are shown in the first column of this table. The American Century was at its height. Truman was in the White House. The United States was again at war, after a scant half-decade of peace. Yet the land of the free was thriving. Looking back from the angry 2020s, Andrews was astonished at how distant it all seemed, how relatively cheerful and hopeful, almost storybook-simple. Time takes its toll, though. Not all the trend-lines would hold.

	1950	1960	1970	1980	1990	2000	2010	2020
Per Capita GDP (a)	$15,559	$19,614	$25,973	$32,377	$40,361	$49,911	$53,683	$62,333
Inflation	$1.00	$1.23	$1.61	$3.42	$5.43	$7.16	$9.06	$10.75
National Debt (b)	76%	43%	35%	31%	52%	55%	87%	126%
Defense Spending (b)	5.0%	9.0%	8%	5.1%	5.6%	3.1%	4.9%	3.7%
Life Expectancy	68	70	71	74	75	77	78	79
Birth Rate (c)	3.15	3.44	2.38	1.79	1.96	2.01	1.98	1.78
Born to Unwed Mothers	5%	7%	13%	21%	26%	33%	41%	41%
Born Outside USA	7%	5%	4%	6%	8%	11%	13%	14%
High School Completion	34%	40%	48%	63%	70%	83%	86%	90%
Church Attendance (d)	39%	49%	40%	40%	40%	42%	38%	31%

a) Constant 2017 dollars
b) Percent of GDP
c) Per woman lifetime
d) At least weekly

CHAPTER TWO
IKE TO JFK TO LBJ

May 1954 – April 1964

That Night in Chicago

Patricia D'Evelyn, whose daughter was to marry John in 1967, with
Goldwater at a campaign event in the early 1960s

He'd never forget the night Senator Goldwater stood down from a bid to wrest the presidential nomination from Vice President Nixon. It was July 1960, and John Andrews had come by train from his summer job in Colorado to serve as a page at the Republican convention in Chicago. The ten minutes of pandemonium that shook the hall after Goldwater was introduced to speak, was like nothing the boy had ever experienced.

The votes weren't there to support a challenge by the valiant Arizonan, everyone knew that; but the GOP Right loved him with a fervor Nixon couldn't come near matching, and his message to the cheering delegates was unmistakable though unspoken: *Keep the faith, stay with me, our day will come.* Which it did, four years later.

Andrews, as he turned 16 that May, hadn't gone looking for a baptism in national politics. Rather, politics had come looking for him, through his father's friendship with industrialist Charles Percy, whose three children had attended the Andrews family's Rocky Mountain camps. Percy, who would later become a U.S. senator from Illinois, was chairing the 1960 Republican platform committee. His twin daughters, Valerie and Sharon, were tapped as convention pages, and when he invited young John to join them, the boy eagerly accepted.

Pinching Himself

It was an instance — one of many — of the theme of this book. Andrews, somewhat in Forrest Gump fashion, repeatedly found himself with a front-row seat at the political parade, more by the agency of others than by his own doing. *Here's your ticket, son. Glad you could join us. Look, here they come.* He had to keep pinching himself. Golly willikers, what luck.

In organizing the book around the successive ten-year periods of the author's life, we necessarily straddle the conventional decades of the Christian calendar with their neat one-word tags, whereby the 1950s were deemed to have been stodgy, the 1960s stormy, so on and so forth. But that's for the best, because the neat tags leave out so much.

John wasn't a month into his second decade, and the '50s not yet half over, when two momentous events occurred that would seed the storms of the '60s. On May 17, 1954, the Supreme Court's mandate for school desegregation thrust America's long-neglected race problem into the center of our national life, where it would remain from then on. And just a few days previously, on May 7, 1954, the victory of Vietnamese communists over French forces at Dien Bien Phu had begun the slow-motion process of ever-deepening U.S. involvement in Gen. MacArthur's nightmare, an endless land war in Asia.

These two rending issues, one domestic and the other foreign, were to vex and torment American politics for long years to come, framing the context for young Andrews' patriotic coming of age. None of this, however, did he remotely foresee just then. Weightier matters preoccupied him. Would John Sr. find room for his bike in the overloaded green Chevy station wagon when they headed to Fennville for the summer? Could the Cards contend in this year's pennant race? And what of the twin cousins, Heather and David Andrews, newborn to his aunt and uncle that June?

Light Bulb

As the 1950s drew on and his teen years approached, there were light-bulb moments for the boy, sudden realizations of the way things are. He began to see just how big America is; how small the world is; and how young a country we still are.

A vast new horizon opened for him, as wide as the continent itself, when his father gambled everything on a Western camp for boys in Buena Vista, Colorado, in 1955 — the fulfillment of a wild, God-glorifying dream that John Sr. had nurtured since his submarine days in the Pacific, a dozen years before. Now, Christian Science families from New York to Los Angeles, Detroit to Dallas, were entrusting their sons to Johnnie's dad for eight weeks in the summer. The boy reveled in every minute of it.

In 1957, the Andrews quit St. Louis to live year-round at the ranch in Buena Vista. When the Russians put Sputnik in orbit that fall, launching the space race and sending a chill of fear through the Free World, John looked at the globe in Mrs. Roman's 8th-grade classroom with new eyes. Overnight, the planet had shrunk. The two oceans his grandfathers' generation had counted on to keep the United States separate and safe, now seemed to matter little.

The time spans defining his sense of the past and future came in for revision too. Celebrations in 1959 marked 100 years since Colorado's recognition as a territory. Men grew beards and donned period costumes. Historical reenactments enlivened the calendar. It occurred to John that when he was born during World War II, many people were still living who had been born during the Civil War. And when that war started in 1861, many people were still living who had been born during the Revolutionary War.

So it had been less than three long lifetimes from then to now, from Independence Hall to Disneyland. Much had changed in Americans' daily lives since then, to be sure, but there was a lot of history left to happen. Plenty of sights and sounds and surprises in the political parade still awaited his generation. *Look, here they come.*

Government and politics, whether he knew it or not, were getting woven into the fabric of John's life. They were no longer something that just happened "out there." His uncle Ed, by now a Michigan state senator in Lansing, took the awestruck boy onto the Senate floor for a handshake with Gov. G. Mennen Williams (D). During that same family trip, at night they'd hear radio ads beaming across the lake from Wisconsin, touting Bill Proxmire (D) for U.S. Senate.

TV and radio didn't figure much into the family's diet of news, however. That came mostly from home subscriptions to *Time, Life,* the *Christian Science Monitor,* and (after they moved back to St. Louis in 1959) the *St. Louis Post-Dispatch.* From such print sources came his vivid impressions of Richard Nixon's impromptu debate with Nikita Khrushchev in Moscow, and of Fidel Castro toppling the Batista regime in Cuba, during the waning months of the 1950s.

A *Life* magazine article about the growing ranks of cynical, negative-minded teenagers, the so-called "nego movement," became the peg on which John hung his 8th-grade valedictory speech in June 1958. He was by this time the perennial choice of his schoolmates for class president and ultimately, in April 1961, for student body president; but that was owing more to his high marks in academics and demeanor than to any explicit political aspirations or aptitude surfacing as yet.

Republican, but Why?

During the autumn presidential race of 1960, for example, despite his having had a front-row seat when the GOP nominated Nixon, it never occurred to the still rather sheltered boy or his thoroughly apolitical parents that John might somehow volunteer for the Nixon campaign on the ground in Missouri. He kept a mildly interested eye on the contest, watched the returns on election night with a sinking heart, and went out for a long, morose walk under the harvest moon after the race was finally called for John F. Kennedy and the Democrats.

Why was he a Republican, anyway? If put on his oath for an answer next day in Mr. Fisher's American history class, junior year at Principia, he'd have been hard pressed to say just why. His whole family were, for starters, but that was lame. So he would probably have said it was because Republicans were for smaller government, free enterprise, individual rights and responsibilities, and cautious change or, if in doubt, no change at all, thank you.

As for the Democrats, well, they were okay one-on-one. Some of his best pals were Democrats, in fact: Mike Barnes, who went on to become a congressman from Maryland, and Drew Stroud, who'd wind up as a gay poet in Japan. But taking them *en masse*, he felt, Democrats just couldn't really be trusted with power, the awesome power of government in the jet age, the nuclear age.

It seemed to him they were less well-anchored to America's founding principles than the Republicans were. The Declaration of Independence, the Constitution, the Bill of Rights, all of that. Look, Democrats had been, back in the day, Lincoln's opponents, the party of slavery and secession. Enough said.

Yet party labels still seemed unsatisfying to Andrews. They were vague, fuzzy, slippery somehow. At some point in 1961, heading into his senior year in high school, he encountered Barry Goldwater's little book *The Conscience of a Conservative,* and it really spoke to him. For a pick-any-topic term paper in one of his English classes, he wrote on "What's a Liberal, Who's a Conservative?" It got a decent mark, but the teacher chided him for what she considered a whiff of zealotry in the paper. He was rankled at the time. In due course, events would show she hadn't been mistaken.

The Ford Factor

Goldwater's name was in the news as Nixon was then widely deemed politically finished, and the Arizona senator was seen as President Kennedy's likely Republican challenger in 1964. Andrews was intrigued with the prospect, but as he took up his political science major at Principia College in the fall of 1962, he found his true-believing conservative zeal faltering under the skeptical Socratic questions of one professor after another.

It was an immersive dose of the same bitter medicine he had first briefly tasted on a Washington trip the previous spring. A half-minute elevator ride was all it had taken for the congressman hosting Andrews' school group, Principia alumnus John Rousselot of California, to crush some cocksure assertion the kid had made about federal spending. Now he found himself in receipt

Soon to graduate from high school and already hooked on politics, John was profiled in the St. Louis paper, May 1962 of similarly polite-but-unanswerable reality checks day by day from Clayton Ford, James Nietmann, and others on the poli-sci faculty.

Ford, the department chairman, had a pushy, blustering style in the classroom that Andrews didn't enjoy. That owlish face scowling at you with the bifocals down on the end of his nose, that pot belly pushing out through the front of his suitcoat as he strode back and forth, lecturing apodictically, left a sour impression.

Though Ford prided himself on never letting students know his party preference, the kid could sense a smug smell of liberal academia about him. John opted for a double major, politics and business, so that his assigned adviser would be the economics professor Robert Andrews instead of the domineering Clayton Ford. (Robert Andrews was the older brother of John Andrews Sr. The older brother of both was David Andrews, Principia's president. As we saw in Chapter 1, the Andrews were thick on the ground at the proud little school.)

Anyway, those early months of young John's college experience were dominated more by an ill-starred romance, horseplay at his men's dorm, and a bench-warming season of varsity football than by political preoccupations of the left or the right. By not being fully in Prof. Ford's orbit, he was spared the departmental ritual of volunteering for the local congressman, liberal Republican Paul Findley.

The only congressional race the kid cared about that fall was the one in southwestern Michigan, where his mother's brother, Edward Hutchinson, won a bid for the U.S. House, a seat he would hold until 1976. In the national results, John took passing note of Nixon's humiliating defeat for governor of California. A spent force for sure, it seemed; no one could doubt it now.

Gunshots in Dallas

That was a jittery time for Americans, for the whole world, in fact, with the Cuban Missile Crisis having ended just a week or two before. Andrews hoped and prayed mankind would never again come so close to nuclear Armageddon. He didn't dream—no one did—that President Kennedy's fraught entanglement with communist Cuba would cost JFK his life barely one year later, November 22, 1963, when gunshots rang out in Dallas.

Nineteen sixty-three's other momentous events that would change history were largely lost on the kid, however. He had fences to mend with his father at camp that summer, and a soccer team to conjure into being at his college that fall. George Wallace in Alabama obstructing black students, Martin Luther King Jr. in Washington appealing for racial equality, Ngo Dinh Diem in Saigon struck down by his own inner circle: none of it really shook John, until that day when LBJ was suddenly the president, the only president we had, and John's attention snapped back to the present.

Those final weeks of 1963 were something of a turning point for him. The least a fellow can do, if favored with a front-row seat on history, is to keep eyes front and gratefully absorb as much meaning, as much benefit from the spectacle as possible. And from then on, across the decades and really without interruption down to the present day, such became John Andrews' unflagging endeavor.

An even more important turning point for the kid, really a life-changing moment, came in the early weeks of 1964. For almost a year he had been socially unattached, "playing the field" as they used to call it. On a snowy night in March, he idly decided to drop in on a no-date dance at the college gym. Never much of a dancer, he undertook to shuffle a couple of times around the floor with a lissome California blonde he knew from one of his classes and before that from camp, Donna D'Evelyn. Lightning struck.

In the coming days, he realized she was all he had ever wanted in a girl. Indeed, in her quick empathy with his scarcely half-formed conservative beliefs and ideals, Donna was more than John had dreamt of. She "got" him as no one ever had, and they were soon inseparable. Never again would Andrews lack for a soulmate to mirror his fascination with the political parade.

And he was stirred, now, to participate as well as spectate, for her parents, Mort and Patty D'Evelyn, were deep-dyed movement conservatives, steeped in grassroots activism. Their fervent civic spirit gradually invested him, through her, as the young couple fell in love.

Was anyone in the GOP going to be able to stop Senator Goldwater? Or would it even matter, given the increasingly unstoppable force that was President Johnson? Such were the questions parade-watchers were asking themselves as Andrews' second decade concluded in the spring of 1964.

Ironically, as the senator's Republican support grew, the kid had cooled toward him. Predictable: the sophomoric impulse to rethink all received ideas was strong. Yet the decade had been another amply grateful one for John; no rethinking on that score.

To come of age in any era, anywhere, was wondrous in itself. And more so, perforce, in an America outgrowing year by year its brief, heady postwar preeminence and contending with unaccustomed limits in an uneasy homeland and an unruly world. So many unknowns; so much at stake. It filled him with sobering pride, this realization that his country, *his fatherland,* carried the hopes of mankind. He was determined to do his part.

VITAL SIGNS, 1960

"Get this country moving again." So went the Kennedy for President slogan in 1960. Closing his eyes and tuning out the political noise of mid-2024, John Andrews could hear the JFK rhetoric in that flat Boston accent as if it were yesterday.

It was a smart generational play for the Democratic nominee, brimming with energy and so much younger than the grandfatherly Republican he hoped to replace. But the 1960 numbers (table, second column) tell a different story. Real income was up 25 percent in a decade. Birth rates, education levels, and longevity were up.

The debt burden was down and defense spending was up—Kennedy's allegations of a "missile gap" notwithstanding. It even appeared Americans were praying more, just as President Eisenhower had urged. Andrews was coming of age in a nation with bright prospects, it would seem.

	1950	1960	1970	1980	1990	2000	2010	2020
Per Capita GDP (a)	$15,559	$19,614	$25,973	$32,377	$40,361	$49,911	$53,683	$62,333
Inflation	$1.00	$1.23	$1.61	$3.42	$5.43	$7.16	$9.06	$10.75
National Debt (b)	76%	43%	35%	31%	52%	55%	87%	126%
Defense Spending (b)	5.0%	9.0%	8%	5.1%	5.6%	3.1%	4.9%	3.7%
Life Expectancy	68	70	71	74	75	77	78	79
Birth Rate (c)	3.15	3.44	2.38	1.79	1.96	2.01	1.98	1.78
Born to Unwed Mothers	5%	7%	13%	21%	26%	33%	41%	41%
Born Outside USA	7%	5%	4%	6%	8%	11%	13%	14%
High School Completion	34%	40%	48%	63%	70%	83%	86%	90%
Church Attendance (d)	39%	49%	40%	40%	40%	42%	38%	31%

a) Constant 2017 dollars; b) Percent of GDP; c) Per woman lifetime; d) At least weekly

CHAPTER THREE
LBJ TO NIXON

May 1964 – April 1974

The Speech Unspoken

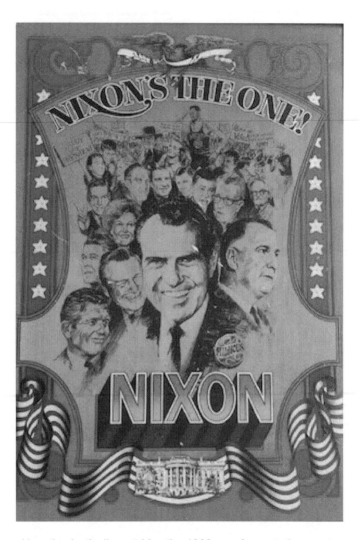

Unenthusiastically watching the 1968 race from wartime posts in the far Pacific, Doc and Ork decided Nixon was probably the one for them

A part of him could never stop wondering if the speech he worked on to help Nixon escape the Watergate scandal—a sort of Checkers II, contrite, disarming—would have worked, had the president gone ahead and given it.

It was the summer of 1973. Young John Andrews, earthling, improbably found himself in the political stratosphere as a member of President Richard Nixon's speechwriting staff. Reelected the previous year in a massive landslide, Nixon was now in deep and perhaps fatal trouble with prosecutorial and congressional bloodhounds baying on his trail over a bungled campaign-spying scheme at Democratic headquarters in the Watergate building a few blocks from the White House.

Handlers believed the beleaguered president could put the scandal to rest with one bracingly candid speech appealing to the American people over the heads of the liberal media and an adversarial Washington establishment. Nixon had pulled it off before, after all; his nationally televised "Checkers" speech had saved the earnest, combative Californian from being thrown off the ticket by Eisenhower in 1952. Why not again?

Chief speechwriter Raymond Price tapped Andrews for the high-stakes assignment this time. He was to gather input from the two senior staffers closest to the president, national security adviser Henry Kissinger and press secretary Ron Ziegler, work up a first draft, then start the revising and polishing process with Nixon himself.

The project died aborning, however. Where Kissinger urged a contrite tone (which John also favored, but what did he know), Ziegler insisted on unapologetic defiance. The two opposite approaches couldn't possibly be melded into one speech. Checkers II wasn't attempted. Watergate became a death spiral, and in less than a year, Nixon was forced to resign. Andrews, his spirit broken, was gone in half a year.

Swamped

Well, not altogether broken in spirit, but severely bruised and battered; that would more accurately describe John's state of mind as 1974 came in. He had invested a lot emotionally — a lot — in President Nixon and Vice President Agnew. Now it was all crashing down. And the ugly spectacle of seeing the voters' decisive verdict annulled by gutter tactics in mere months made him sick.

Besides, this whole decade had been a headlong rush of momentous life-changes for the young idealist. This final, cruel twist understandably left him numb and drained. The years since 1964 had seen him become a college honor graduate, then a naval officer, then a husband and father, then a gung-ho White House staffer, and now a political refugee of sorts, turning his back on Washington and New York to essay a new start in the Rocky Mountains, of all places.

Charging ahead in one role after another, he was all the while conscious of a need to work out exactly what it was he believed, but it seemed events moved so quickly there was never the luxury of slowing down enough to do that. Case in point: Goldwater for President, way back in 1964.

Though Donna was all for Barry, John was less and less sure. While she was volunteering at the GOP convention in San Francisco, he had spent the summer in Europe, viewing U.S. politics through the supercilious liberal lens of the *International Herald Tribune*. Back on campus in the fall, the prevailing leftish atmosphere — yes, even that long ago, even at a little church college in the Illinois cornfields — operated on him. Was this a process of growing up, or of selling out? He squirmed, but wasn't all that sorry when Lyndon Johnson swamped Goldwater on election night.

More painful, because more personal, was getting swamped himself the following spring in a race for student body president that he thought was in the bag. He set his sights on a summer of civil rights work in the South, but his father vetoed that. Failure was unfamiliar. Being told no was unpleasant. Might the kid need to reinvent himself? Finally in the fall of 1965, his senior year, he began to find his footing again.

Investigating the cynical sleight of hand by real-estate brokers that had long kept St. Louis neighborhoods segregated, for his capstone project in political science, he landed a private interview with Missouri governor Warren Hearnes. Angling for a Rhodes Scholarship, he made it as far as the state finals. His bond with Donna deepened when she helped him win a campus-wide vote to adopt a new honor code for the college.

At an all-students convocation shortly before graduating, he gave a paper entitled "The Elsah Manifesto," arguing that Principia, grounded on the Bible, should embody a truer radicalism than anything the young political Left had to offer. The cool assurance that they could remake America overnight, top to bottom, with far superior results was one aspect of his generation's boundless narcissism. Andrews detested that Baby Boomer cult of self-adulation, yet couldn't help partaking of it in some degree.

Would he push upstream against the current of the times, or swim with it? To follow his father's and grandfather's naval tradition, as he set out to do in November 1966, and then to marry his college sweetheart as he did in April 1967, showed that John was hardly prey to the "Burn it all down" nihilism of SDS and SNCC, Che Guevara and Mao.

Kirk, Burke, Buckley

Yet the young submariner's after-hours fascination with notions of a "spiritual revolution" to be loosed on the world any day now by his unorthodox Christian Science faith, bespoke a nonconformist soul behind the conventional exterior. Had some of the restlessness that kept his father forever on the move, with visionary ministry endeavors and footloose nomadic travel, been passed down to the son in the form of ever-evolving blueprints for political and religious castles in the air? Certainly at this stage John Andrews' conservatism, if you could call it that, wasn't exactly standard-issue Russell Kirk or Edmund Burke.

He did, however, get a chance to introduce himself to Kirk's illustrious disciple, William F. Buckley Jr., when the conservative firebrand and *National Review* founder spoke at the University of Hawaii near John's duty station at Pearl Harbor in 1968. Buckley expressed a kindly interest in the kid's aspirations and urged him to stay in touch — which he was to do, very beneficially, in the coming years.

Andrews had become an avid reader of *National Review* since learning of it from Donna's brother, the intense, brilliant Tom D'Evelyn. Nineteen sixty-eight would be the first presidential election he could vote in, and he hungrily took in the magazine's rigorous application of constitutional principles to practical politics amid the chaotic events of that year.

As Vietnam became a quagmire and riots rocked the cities, he and his countrymen saw LBJ abjure reelection, Martin

Luther King Jr. and Robert Kennedy felled by assassins' bullets — and the electrifying Ronald Reagan bested for the Republican nomination by an uninspiring Richard Nixon, while Vice President Hubert Humphrey won the Democratic nod at a strife-torn convention in Chicago.

The kid's closest friend from school days, Allen Orcutt, now a Marine helicopter pilot, stopped through Honolulu enroute back to Oklahoma from Vietnam for emergency leave. As between Nixon and Humphrey, both agreed the Republican would have their vote. But neither thought it would make much difference, given the mess America was in. John, or Doc as Allen affectionately called him, little dreamt what a difference Nixon was to make in his own life — and in turning the country around.

It was a strange time to be serving in uniform. While the United States was surely at war, Andrews and his shipmates were not, not in the slightest. Submarines weren't needed to fight this pajama-clad enemy. Helicopters were, though, and Orcutt was very much at war. The U.S. commitment to keeping South Vietnam free would cost him his marriage (the reason for that emergency leave) and ultimately his life. One of their college friends, Pete Gans, was shot all to pieces over there. Another, John Sweet, was shot dead. For what?

It was America's second bloody and bitter, but half-hearted and inconclusive, military engagement in as many decades. Seeing Ork off at the airport, Doc was choked with feelings of doubt, dread, and disgust — emotions he'd not be able to put into words until years later, pangs of sorrow at the tragedy overtaking not only his dear friend but his beloved country. The political parade they had speculated about was still dimly visible to his mind's eye in the warm autumn darkness. But it held no glitter for him that night.

Grinding

On February 25, 1969, at Tripler Army Hospital near the Pearl Harbor submarine base, Donna gave birth to a baby girl, Christina Hill Andrews. John was beside himself with wonder and delight. This was the reason for it all! This was why politics were practiced, oceans crossed, isles and continents settled, armies and navies dispatched, wars waged — not for the high drama and glitter of it, but so that ordinary folk like this wide-eyed young couple could live their ordinary lives and bring this extraordinary thing, new life, into the undeserving world.

Far away in Washington, meanwhile, wheels were turning that would set John Andrews on a startling new course before the year was out. A public-relations man named Gene Bradley, another in John's father's seemingly endless string of useful connections acquired through the Colorado camps, had been favorably impressed with the kid's Elsah Manifesto and now proposed to recruit him for a plum writing assignment pitched at a national audience.

General Electric, a client of Bradley's, was devoting the next issue of its quarterly magazine, *GE Forum*, to the competing visions of America's young radicals. Must the "system," the status quo so bitterly reviled by the civil rights and antiwar movements, be torn down — or could we improve it and save it? Famed activist Carl Oglesby, a leader in the Students for a Democratic Society, would argue from the left. Arguing from the right, if willing, would be none other than Lieutenant (j.g.) John K. Andrews Jr., USNR.

Willing? Need you ask? John toiled over the piece in every spare moment for weeks; ginned up a little photo shoot with some church friends, Dave and Susie Howell, for ostensibly candid illustrations; and fought off the usual authorial qualms about his turgid prose and his manifest unfitness for the whole wretched project. Finally, into the mail it went, and he ended up not feeling half bad about it.

In grinding out this article he had accomplished, in spite of himself, the long-postponed imperative of figuring out what he most deeply believed, this side of heaven. Namely, he believed in the supreme validity of the truths and principles of the American founding, as expressed in the Declaration of Independence and the Constitution of the United States. This now became a settled, unshakable conviction that was to guide him infallibly for the rest of his life. The pleasant sensation of being on a magazine cover was fleeting; this was for keeps.

Andrews had scarcely gotten over the surprise from Gene Bradley when he received another surprise from Uncle Sam, and they turned out to be linked. His active-duty Navy obligation, contracted to last until November 1970, was abruptly shortened by a year. He'd now be a civilian again as of November 1969—and in need of a job. Enter, yet again, his father's uncanny network of friends.

John Ehrlichman, a top adviser to President Nixon, had sent his son to the Colorado camp. Learning that John Andrews Jr. wanted to go into journalism, and aware of the *GE Forum* article, he asked to see the kid's resume. Ehrlichman wrote back to inform John he had given the resume to two White House colleagues: communications director Herb Klein, who was circulating it to friendly newspaper editors, and press secretary Ron Ziegler, who might be needing a junior staffer. Andrews got a good laugh out of the latter. *Me in the White House press office. Right!*

Starstruck

Washington didn't remotely figure into John's aims and hopes right then. When Jim Blanchard, his skipper aboard U.S.S. *Bonefish*, looking to keep him in the Navy, offered him a coveted post at the Pentagon as aide to the Vice Chief of Naval Operations, he politely declined without a second thought. Though smiling inside, Andrews would soon learn the joke was on him.

Before Thanksgiving, Ron Ziegler reached him by phone in Kansas City, where John was just days away from starting a newspaper job; some persuasive lobbying by fellow Principian and Ehrlichman staffer Bud Krogh was applied; and presto, the press secretary made the hire. On January 20, 1970, a starstruck Johnnie A was assigned a desk in the stairwell a few paces from the Cabinet Room and set about learning the ropes in White House media relations.

It was one year to the day after President Nixon took office, and a tumultuous year it had been. With Vietnam casualties worsening despite Lyndon Johnson's having been evicted from power, the American left decided this was Richard Nixon's war now, and he must be made to feel the heat for its unpopularity.

For Andrews, 1969 had been far less about the political than the personal—doting on a new baby daughter, marveling at the moon landing, navigating the complexities of a return to the mainland and civilian life. But for the Republican president, the year had been a cauldron of troubles. The Left, having broken one president in the spring of 1968 and shattered his party later that summer, now undertook to break another president in the fall of 1969, besieging the nation's capital with hundreds of thousands of raging demonstrators.

Nixon had rallied the country with his masterful "Silent Majority" speech, setting the opposition back on their heels for the moment, but no one doubted they would be at him again soon enough, and in force. The kid, starchily self-conscious in his suit and tie, showing up bright and early each day to help the Leader of the Free World get his message out, sensed an ever-present tension just below the shiny surface of presidential pomp and circumstance. Intoxicating as all the power and glory were, the whole thing seemed hanging by a thread.

But to get the pulse of this behemoth, the federal government, with its three sprawling branches, its vast resources, and its huge impact on American life—to grasp the manifold purposes, priorities, and personalities of a presidential administration—Andrews could have had no more perfect vantage point than the White House press office. Through this one node must pass everything and everyone connected with Mr. Nixon's vision for the country during his time in power. The kid took it all in with great gulps of information, impressions, and insights.

And having little choice but to plunge, he plunged. Whether in impersonating Ziegler to answer his mail, or in ordering Cabinet officers about by their first names at a news conference, or in blithely jetting around the country as part of the Air Force One entourage, he felt himself taking on a confident persona hitherto unimaginable. It was true what C. S. Lewis says, he found: play-acting, kept up long enough, can change one for real. Or in the vernacular: "Fake it till you make it."

Taking Sides

April and May of 1970 saw the nation swept up in a new firestorm of protest, shock, and recriminations as Nixon, merely trying not to lose the war, was accused of widening it into Cambodia — after which, panicky riot-control measures cost the lives of six students in Ohio and Mississippi, and hard-hat construction workers confronted antiwar demonstrators in New York.

It began to feel as if the whole world was choosing up sides, and it got personal for John Andrews when his college soccer buddy Bill Foster, now a grad student at Columbia, phoned to say he was driving down to picket the White House and could he crash on the Andrews' couch. *Sorry, maybe another time,* was the kid's answer.

Again as in the crisis of the previous autumn, all of this failed to break the president, but it profoundly shook him. He ventured out of the White House in the wee hours of the night for a few minutes of dialogue with young protesters at the Lincoln Memorial. He warned plaintively in a national television address that America must not be reduced to "a pitiful, helpless giant." Andrews winced.

Nixon was a political brawler when he had to be, though. The hard-hats roaring in Wall Street were the Silent Majority finding its voice. Why not bid to take back the Senate? He had been the first president in more than a hundred years to take office with both houses of Congress in opposition hands. It was impeding his Vietnam withdrawal, and had already cost him two Supreme Court nominees, Haynsworth and Carswell. Republicans would need to pick up seven seats, a heavy lift; but stranger things have happened. (In the event, after a raucous campaign, they gained only two — but to John's delight, one of them was James Buckley, Bill's brother.)

In the press secretary's office, meanwhile, the pace never slackened. He took Andrews along on presidential trips to Mexico, Bermuda, Ireland, Italy, Spain, and Yugoslavia. To watch Nixon pay court to Franco in Madrid and Tito in Belgrade was to see a generational handoff of power; two old warhorses of the 1930s and '40s about to exit the stage. One such *did* exit on the very day they got to Yugoslavia: word came that Nasser of Egypt had died.

Recently promoted to the speechwriting staff, John brought in his parents and Donna for a Rose Garden photo with the President

Ron Ziegler was not an easy man to work for, John was finding. To act as a sort of valet to him on these trips was the least of it. Self-important, irritable, vain, in over his head, he wasn't always sure what he wanted from staffers — but dammit, he wanted it *now*. Yet even in such humdrum duties as answering the boss's mail, opportunity lurked. The kid discovered he had an aptitude for ghost-writing. He could pretend he was someone else and put the illusion across on paper.

The brilliant Daniel Patrick Moynihan, later to be a Democratic senator from New York (after ousting Jim Buckley), but for now Nixon's in-house policy intellectual, liked to send the press secretary little jocular memos, sparkling with wit and erudition. It fell to Andrews to answer these in Ziegler's name. For John it was like batting around a tennis ball with Arthur Ashe, a rookie writer's fiery baptism.

Soon he was tasked with a bigger assignment. Dwight Chapin, one of Ron Ziegler's staff pals, had been a 1969 recipient of an award called the Ten Outstanding Young Men of America. "I'd like to be one of their 1970 honorees, John," came the marching orders. "Can you make it happen, kid?"

To be called "kid" by Ziegler, barely five years his senior, always made the kid's blood boil. But he took up the challenge and landed the win, after weeks of multi-identity ghosting, pushy networking, and wheeler-dealering with well-connected Nixon backers.

Even with that feather in his cap, however, Andrews was getting on so poorly with Ziegler that he fully expected to be fired as 1970 waned. Instead, failing upward, he was transferred to the speechwriting office, where chief editor Raymond Price wanted someone under 30 in the lineup as the campuses seethed and the 18-year-old vote came on. The kid checked all the boxes: able to fog a mirror, reasonably fluent in English, and still hopelessly boyish at 26. Nineteen seventy-one rolled in with a whole new universe of possibilities.

Bully Pulpit

Now began the first of three brief chapters in Andrews' life when he was truly *in*, not just *at*, the grand political parade of our times. Not again until the 1990s, with his run for governor and his election to the state Senate, would he taste the exhilaration of actively mixing in the march of events.

Command of the written and spoken word is the most decisive advantage in a president's exercise of power. This is what Lincoln meant when he said that public sentiment is everything. It is what Theodore Roosevelt meant when he talked of the bully pulpit. Indeed, it's what St. Paul was getting at when he warned that a great cause cannot succeed with an uncertain trumpet.

Success for President Nixon's endeavor to reunite a divided nation and give peace a chance in the world would require best efforts day by day from Ray Price and his little stable of writers. Flanking Price, the moderate, thoughtful, steady Yale man, were Patrick Buchanan, hard right, street fighter, a pen on fire, and William Safire, liberal pragmatist, dry wit, worldly wise, urbane. On the next tier down from this big three were David Gergen, Lee Huebner, John McLaughlin, Tex Lezar, and a handful of other journeymen, now joined by John Andrews.

The kid got off to a rough start as he struggled to learn the difference between writing for the eye and writing for the ear. But he loved the work and thrived under Price's kindly tutelage. It was sink or swim. You'd better be versatile, agile, thick-skinned, and a quick study, or the place would eat you alive.

Speech topics ranged widely over all sorts of issues. For policy expertise John might work with Chuck Colson on school vouchers, Peter Flanigan on finance, John Whitaker on environment, Leonard Garment on civil rights, Bud Krogh on law enforcement, or Henry Kissinger on foreign policy.

Kissinger's deputy, Gen. Alexander Haig—later to be Nixon's chief of staff, then Reagan's secretary of state— personally showed Andrews around West Point. The course of John's duties also took him to the Western White House in San Clemente and the presidential retreat at Camp David (so named by Ike in the 1950s for his grandson, David Eisenhower, who married Nixon's daughter Julie in 1969). Sometimes the kid would work directly with the president on drafting a speech, as when Nixon delivered the eulogy for J. Edgar Hoover, legendary FBI director.

It was a better year for Nixon, 1971, than his first two had been. He was on offense now and meant to stay there. Vietnamization was taking hold, casualties were down, and troops were coming home. John Connally, the charismatic Texas Democrat, was named treasury secretary and ran point when wage and price controls were imposed to curb inflation. And then Richard Nixon stunned the world by announcing he would visit Communist China in early 1972. Holy cow.

But wait. China rapprochement? Price controls? Was this how conservatives did things? Absolutely not, said Bill Buckley and Pat Buchanan. It felt wrong to John Andrews too, but he said nothing. Was there a greater good to be served, triangulating Beijing against Moscow, resetting the global chess board, forestalling a return to power by the Kennedys (Teddy this time, damaged by Chappaquiddick, but still a force to be feared)? The kid held his tongue, did his job, and kept his head down.

Termites

Politically things were breaking in the president's favor as the 1972 election took shape. His Democratic challenger seemed likely to be the quixotic Sen. George McGovern of South Dakota, not the formidable Sen. Edward Kennedy of Massachusetts. He faced only token opposition in the GOP primaries from two little-known congressmen, Pete McCloskey of California and John Ashbrook of Ohio. He dominated the headlines with his China trip in February and the Moscow Summit in May.

The imposing edifice that was to be a transformative, eight-year, presumed Age of Nixon had termites in the rafters, however. The roof was destined to fall in when extra-legal clandestine activities by a few White House staff were sensationally brought to light over the course of an agonizing two-year ordeal for Nixon beginning in June 1972.

Of course all this was undreamt of by the young John Andrews as he traveled with the presidential party to the Soviet Union via Austria, Iran, and Poland just before Memorial Day. His task for the week, under Dr. Kissinger's watchful eye, was to craft the speech Nixon would give to a joint session of Congress upon returning from the trip. Bill Safire was brought along to handle daily writing chores as the itinerary took them not only to Moscow but also to Leningrad and Kiev. Andrews lapped up the old pro's stories of his last time here with Nixon in 1959,

Andrews, right, was low man on the writing staff. Ray Price, 4th from left, led the team. His big guns were William Safire, 2nd from left, and Patrick Buchanan, 5th from right

when the then vice president had sparred lustily with Nikita Khrushchev in their famous impromptu "Kitchen Debate."

After John shook hands with Leonid Brezhnev, Khrushchev's successor and the man who had crushed the Prague Spring with tanks in 1968, at the opening-night dinner in the Kremlin, he mused ironically on which was morally called for: never to wash that hand again, or to wash it until the skin was raw and all taint of the brutal dictator's touch was gone. No contest, he concluded: it must be the latter.

What would prove impossible for the president to wash off, though, was the taint of criminality from zealots acting in his name amid the superheated atmosphere of protecting national security at all costs and winning a second term whatever it took.

At the very moment on June 1st when Nixon was receiving an ovation in Congress for his address about the Summit — drafted by Andrews — operatives from his campaign were planting wiretaps in Democratic offices at the Watergate. When they were caught during a second burglary there on June 17th, it was the beginning of the end for the 37th president of the United States.

But all of this would unfold in the slowest of slow motion, and for the rest of 1972 Mr. Nixon, to all appearances, was going from strength to strength. At the Republican convention in Miami, John and Donna basked in the reflected glow of RN's coronation and preened themselves on being on the insider list for various social functions — a flattering contrast to their lowly status as student observers at the Chicago convention in 1960 (for him) and the San Francisco convention in 1964 (for her).

He contributed a paragraph or two to the president's acceptance speech (which are always, like State of the Union addresses, written by committee), and as the campaign barreled ahead he had the fun of seeing, on one occasion, a gag line he'd suggested for the Boss get used in preference to one submitted by Bob Hope's writers — and on another occasion, his recommendation of a Bible verse to garnish some speech get picked up in preference to one that Billy Graham's people had sent in.

Ray Price insisted his writers maintain "a passion for anonymity" with no public claiming of credit. Still there was quiet satisfaction in finding that one could rub elbows with the famous and sometimes scratch out at least a single off big-league pitching.

On election day aboard Air Force One, as the Nixon team flew back to Washington from California, the kid had the thrill of chatting with the great Theodore H. White, whose *Making of the President* books since 1960 had become a sort of political bible to him. On the ground below, Americans were awarding RN a 49-state landslide. A bright future seemed to beckon.

Unmaking

Be careful what you wish for. The political parade in 1973 was to become, for John Andrews, a grim experience devoid of glamor. Not the making but the unmaking of a president would be sadly chronicled in Teddy White's next book, *Breach of Faith*.

Yes, January saw Nixon sworn in for another term; the cessation of hostilities with North Vietnam, including return of the POWs; and the opening skirmishes of what the administration was calling the Battle of the Budget, a massive effort to rein in federal spending. All of which Andrews relished. But then things went south.

Whether as a result of some secret meeting where decisions were reached or (more likely) as a spontaneous determination of the hive mind of the Left, the doom was pronounced: *Nixon Must Go*—at which the vast unseen machinery silently cranked into motion and the inexorable process of taking him down began. Lest we be misunderstood, two things, not then apparent to the woefully naïve Andrews, but clearly seen now, must be stressed:

(1) The anarchic Marxian movement bent on breaking presidents, previously a political fringe element when it brought down LBJ in 1968, had now made its way into the political mainstream by seizing the Democratic Party and its media allies *en bloc.* Its power to do harm thus became vastly greater.

(2) The Nixon men's misdeeds were not nothing; far from it. RN had in fact given his enemies the sword they used to fell him, as he admitted to interviewer David Frost years later. Yet the opposition had options short of destroying him. John Marini's book *Unmasking the Administrative State,* and Geoff Shepard's three books spelling out *The Nixon Conspiracy,* would finally explain, decades later, why the deep state simply could not tolerate the continuance in office of this dangerous — to its own corrupt self-interest, not to the public weal — and dedicated American patriot of the old school.

Bookshelves by the yard, as well as audio and video archives by the hundred hours, now exist to tell all sides of the Watergate saga. It needs no retelling here. Andrews watched from the front row in horror and morbid fascination. Into the hungry maw of criminal prosecution went John Ehrlichman, Bob Haldeman, Bud Krogh, Chuck Colson, John Mitchell, John Dean, and many others, less for the sake of meting out justice to them as individuals than as sacrificial offerings on the altar of "Get Nixon."

The carnage put an end to any jaunty persona of himself as "the kid." Andrews grew up and sobered up overnight, like an untried boy soldier blooded for the first time in combat. And he found that speechwriting for someone you no longer believe in is a hard slog. His muse was utterly gone.

Soon after the Checkers II project was aborted, Andrews was personally coached by the president on how to frame Vice President Spiro Agnew's nationally televised resignation speech over bribery charges in his home state of Maryland. That did it.

Nauseated by the whole tawdry melodrama, Andrews began actively looking for the exit. He quietly sought counsel not only from his mentor, Ray Price, but also from Bill Buckley, Republican national chairman George H. W. Bush, and Rep. Edward Hutchinson, his uncle, who as ranking minority member of the House Judiciary Committee would be in the thick of any impeachment proceedings.

At the Barricades

On December 7, 1973 — a fitting date, he thought, and the very day Rep. Gerald Ford was sworn in to replace Agnew — he left the White House staff. A month later, with publication of a long first-person account in the *Washington Post*, John Andrews' departure from the administration became the only public protest resignation in the entire Watergate affair.

Over the next few weeks he would also speak out in the *New York Times* and *Newsweek*, as well as on CBS News and PBS *Washington Week*. He believed in Nixon's policies but no longer in Nixon, went the argument. He saw Nixon as culpable not legally but ethically; more by acts of omission than commission. The honorable course, he said, would be for the president to resign. Failing that, impeach him.

Call it Johnnie A at the barricades. What to make of this defiant stance? Was it the act of a turncoat, a dupe, a disloyal ingrate, an insolent young pup getting above himself? Or was it a principled, courageous, patriotic position to take?

Andrews at the time, mustering as much honest introspection as he could, hoped for the latter but couldn't altogether discount the former. There remained, and would remain as the decades passed, a degree of squirm. Where he would at last come out in 2023, exactly half a century after the 18-minute tape gap, the Saturday Night Massacre, and "I am not a crook," was that if given a chance to do it all again he would have just kept his mouth shut.

Not that his personal *J'accuse* ended up mattering one iota in whether Nixon would go or stay. But he had wanted it to matter — and looking back after all these years, he ruefully saw himself in the wrong. The John Andrews of 1974 had cast in his lot with the forces <u>that</u> — posture as they might for the moral high ground on the narrow question of whether Nixon had obstructed justice — wished ill to the founding principles of our country, the U.S. Constitution, and the American way of life *tout court*.

Put more simply: Andrews '74, with all his burning idealism and (admit it) hankering for the limelight, had donned the wrong team jersey. Not your finest hour, Johnnie A.

After exploring various job possibilities that would keep him in the East — be it with Bill Buckley at *National Review*, James Buckley at the Senate, Henry Kissinger at the State Department, or even (God help us) something at the *Washington Post* or the Sierra Club — John cast his gaze toward the West and joined the staff of Adventure Unlimited, his father's youth ministry based in Denver.

Springtime in the Rockies found him and Donna, along with Tina, 5; Jennifer, 3; and Daniel, 6 months, settling into a new home at a mile high and a new career-chapter two time zones removed from the Washington swamp. Closing out the third decade of his life, he rang in May on a snowshoe trip in the Colorado back country with Allen Orcutt, his old Marine Corps buddy now also working for Adventure Unlimited.

Had you asked him right then, Andrews would probably have predicted his front-row days were over for good. No matter; he had already seen more of the political parade close up at 30 than most Americans would see in twice or three times that long. And he felt grateful for all of it, the Watergate debacle notwithstanding. Ugly some of it may have been, but America had proven her resiliency, her mettle, across this stormy span of years. What a blessing, he told himself, to have been born at this time and in this place. A fellow could have done worse; far worse.

VITAL SIGNS, 1970

LBJ's heavy commitment to both the Vietnam War and his Great Society welfare programs created a classic "guns and butter" economic squeeze ahead of 1970. Andrews wasn't surprised to see that inflation had heated up during that decade, though the debt burden was still on a healthy downtrend (table, third column).

Out-of-wedlock births having nearly doubled, and the overall birth rate falling sharply, attested that the sexual revolution was taking its toll. There would be a price to pay.

Material prosperity alone wouldn't forever defer the ill-effects of widespread self-indulgence, manifested in disordered families and a debauched currency. In the coming decade John was to redirect his efforts accordingly, less in the realm of votes and more in the realm of values.

	1950	1960	1970	1980	1990	2000	2010	2020
Per Capita GDP (a)	$15,559	$19,614	**$25,973**	$32,377	$40,361	$49,911	$53,683	$62,333
Inflation	$1.00	$1.23	$1.61	$3.42	$5.43	$7.16	$9.06	$10.75
National Debt (b)	76%	43%	35%	31%	52%	55%	87%	126%
Defense Spending (b)	5.0%	9.0%	8%	5.1%	5.6%	3.1%	4.9%	3.7%
Life Expectancy	68	70	71	74	75	77	78	79
Birth Rate (c)	3.15	3.44	2.38	1.79	1.96	2.01	1.98	1.78
Born to Unwed Mothers	5%	7%	13%	21%	26%	33%	41%	41%
Born Outside USA	7%	5%	4%	6%	8%	11%	13%	14%
High School Completion	34%	40%	48%	63%	70%	83%	86%	90%
Church Attendance (d)	39%	49%	40%	40%	40%	42%	38%	31%

a) Constant 2017 dollars
b) Percent of GDP
c) Per woman lifetime
d) At least weekly

CHAPTER FOUR
FORD TO CARTER TO REAGAN

May 1974 – April 1984

For the Gipper, Eventually

Hillsdale president George Roche boosted the college
to national prominence via his CCA issue seminars on
campus, the ever-growing Imprimis list, and eventually
the Shavano Institute roadshow

Looking back, it was sort of embarrassing, the fact he had been on Team Bush instead of Team Reagan in the runup to 1980. On the other hand, that did fit the Andrews mold. So much of what happened to him at the political parade was improvised, unplanned. Why did John, at some point in 1979, sign up with a loose-knit "theme and message advisory group" on the George Bush for President campaign? Simply because Dave Gergen called and asked him to.

The sum total of his contributions amounted to one or two memos of less-than-brilliant brainstorming about how to evict President Carter from the White House and elect Bush. In after years he would conclude that Reagan was worth ten of Bush in terms of the two men's impact on history. But the centrist Gergen, Ray Price's managing editor in the Nixon speechwriting shop, had remained one of Andrews' touch points in Washington during those Ford and Carter years, and the flattering invite was no sooner offered than accepted.

Truth to tell, John was something of a cheap date politically at that point. Now half a decade removed from the pinnacles of power and largely contented to be so, rewardingly absorbed with his work at the youth organization, he was still far from cured of the stubborn Potomac fever that stays dormant in your blood like malaria. It didn't take much to stir the old juices.

The Bush gig was one of various experiments he undertook at that period, trying new roles on for size, casting about for his calling. There was a contribution he was meant to make for God and country—of that he felt sure—and it was probably something he'd have to invent, not anyone else's standard job description. So far so good. But what was it supposed to look like?

Part of what he needed to sort out in that spring of 1974 was the question of scale, scope, locality. What was the field of action where he could plant his feet, dig in, and start contributing on a human scale? After starting out in Washington when he was so young, and at so high a level, he was now in the odd situation of having to live his political life backwards.

Never mind the lofty self-importance of 1600 Pennsylvania Avenue; what was a Republican precinct caucus all about? Why did it matter who your three county commissioners were? What went on under the gold dome of the Colorado State Capitol?

Breakfast Club

John Andrews began learning the answers by attending political grassroots nursery school, as it were, at the Wednesday breakfast meetings of the Arapahoe County Republican Men's Club in his Denver suburb. Miles Cortez, an attorney he had met at church, introduced him there. State Sen. Hugh Fowler, a Navy man like John, was one of the first to befriend him. A frequent speaker was the local congressman, winsome Bill Armstrong, whom John had first met in Washington in 1972 through the good offices of GOP state chairman (and fellow Christian Scientist) Dwight Hamilton.

On a gray November morning over cold scrambled eggs at a greasy spoon near the county courthouse, the club commiserated the previous night's 1974 election wipeout, when Colorado Democrats capitalized on Watergate to oust the governor and a U.S. senator while flipping one house of the legislature. For Andrews, there was something personal, immediate, and *real* about all this that had never come home to him quite so forcefully in palmy White House days.

The national scene still tugged at him. He took an occasional stab at setting up as a pundit in places like *National Review*, the *Denver Post*, or a short-lived magazine startup called the *Democratic Review*, backed by his high school pal Michael Barnes, later to be a Democratic congressman from Maryland.

On a California trip to see Donna's mother in August 1975, he arranged to pay a courtesy call on former President Nixon at his oceanfront estate in San Clemente. It was a relief to find that RN had either forgiven John's defection from the cause—or perhaps had never even known of it, so isolated was he from much of the news during those final, morose months in office.

At any rate, the writeup of their brief interview landed an Andrews byline in the *Christian Science Monitor*: "Nixon one year after." John felt gratified by this first appearance in the well-regarded, respectably liberal daily paper published by his church. More of his energy was actually being taken up at that time by musing on the spiritual requisites for a free society than by tracking the routine ephemera of governance, and this had started him wrestling in a new way with what this cradle religion of his, this Christian Science, was all about.

Triad

His growing doubts were more than academic, since forming teenagers into the Christian Science way of life was the very essence of his day job at Adventure Unlimited. And then in turn it would only be a matter of time before frictions arose over all of this with John's employer: his father.

Add to this the young couple's shock at the Christian Science–related deaths of her father in 1974 and his mother in 1978, together with long-felt marital tensions worsened by avoidance, and the atmosphere at home was also volatile. Generalities about the American triad of faith, family, and freedom are fine for the Fourth of July. But when two of those three begin to totter, the slogan alone isn't much to build a life on.

Such would be Andrews' view of this in hindsight, anyway. At the time, life tended to roll along with its own momentum, and he would have avowed himself the happiest of men. He loved knocking about the Colorado high country at all seasons, running in 10K races, and coaching youth soccer.

President Ford's defeat in the 1976 election was no surprise, but Colorado Republicans regained some traction, taking back the state House and easily reelecting Congressman Armstrong, for whom John did a bit of surrogate speaking at campaign events. His uncle Ed, Congressman Edward Hutchinson of Michigan, opted to step down that year, handing on his seat to one David Stockman, a young man in a hurry who would go on to become President Reagan's budget director.

All this time Doc (his *nom de guerre* within Adventure Unlimited, to avoid being called John Jr.) was reading voraciously in history, biography, religion, and political thought. No graduate student ever hit the books harder or burned more late oil.

He wanted to understand America and how a free people govern themselves. He wanted to understand social change and why great nations rise and fall. He wanted to understand the Bible and the historic Christian faith. He wanted to understand *ideas*, the bigger the better.

Wilderness

The writing that should logically ensue from so much reading, didn't as yet. There was a file drawer full of overheated monographs on spiritual topics that he showed to no one; but for the most part he simply kept it all in and let it marinate. He began to think of himself as an idea broker—a term he picked up from yet another of Theodore White's books, *In Search of History*.

The forces that would put Ronald Reagan in the White House in 1980 were already stirring in Colorado and across the country during Jimmy Carter's "malaise" years of the late 1970s. Taxpayer revolts broke out in states from Massachusetts to California, with the latter enacting the famous Proposition 13 to cap property taxes. Ripples reached Denver.

Bill Armstrong came from far behind in the polls to defeat Democratic Sen. Floyd Haskell in 1978. But GOP hopes of knocking off popular Gov. Dick Lamm were not to be. Andrews was on the steering committee for one of Lamm's challengers, Lakewood mayor Jim Richey—never dreaming that he would find himself in Richey's shoes a dozen years later.

Near-term in his personal life, however, Doc had allowed dysfunctions to develop that no amount of doctoring could set right. Nineteen eighty into 1981 became the *annus horribilis* when his marriage, his church, and his job all blew up, one after another. He had broken trust with Donna and their children. He had decided Christian Science was false to Scripture. And he had adjudged the man in the mirror, for those reasons, unfit to continue in youth ministry. His stark self-sentence: *Into the wilderness with you, apostate.*

The miracle of God's grace that was John Andrews' eventual marital reconciliation and religious rebirth is a story best told elsewhere. Christ took him in and Donna took him back, suffice to say. Meanwhile, though, even during his bleak time in exile, the drumbeat of the political parade was always there. It drew him back to his native state of Michigan, where a little no-name college in rural Hillsdale was making a stir among conservatives across the land.

Colorado native George Roche, president of Hillsdale College since 1971, had begun putting the place on the map with his defiant refusal of federal aid—and the strings that came with it—and his open door to advocates of liberty and limited government at a time when more and more campuses were making them unwelcome.

Imprimis, the monthly digest of notable speeches given at Hillsdale, was being sent free to a national readership approaching 100,000.

Hugh Fowler had given them some names from the breakfast club, including that of John Andrews. Andrews now, in early 1981, went to see President Roche, inquiring how he might go about launching something similar on the Colorado scene. Suppressing a smile, the quiet-spoken educator gently told him it was a near impossibility.

Starting Shavano

John was bumping along later that year as press secretary to the state Republican Party, under its ebullient chairman,

Bo Callaway, when Dr. Roche's office called to invite him to a confidential weekend meeting in Vail. Sen. Fowler was one of a half dozen others attending. Denver businessmen Chuck Stevinson and John McCarty were the hosts.

George Roche, it developed, after a brilliant decade at Hillsdale, wanted to come home to the Colorado mountains and turn a new page in his career as a force multiplier for conservative thought. The Vail meeting yielded agreement to start something called the Shavano Institute for National Leadership, headed by Roche and staffed by Andrews along with Fowler and others they would recruit.

Seated, L to R, George Roche with Charlton Heston when the movie icon headlined a Shavano event in Denver. Standing, R to L, Shavano staffers Mike Rosen, John Andrews, Allen Orcutt, Jack Solon

Shavano took its name from a high peak on the Continental Divide, rich in frontier lore. They envisioned a sort of Aspen Institute of the Right, convening seminars and retreats where top executives could rediscover America's founding principles. Andrews had found a vehicle for his aspirations as an idea broker. He was to commute between Colorado and Michigan, wearing another hat as the college's manager of guest speakers and editor of *Imprimis*—the trustees having agreed to sponsor the new venture if Roche stayed at Hillsdale as president.

The Shavano Institute years were high adventure for John Andrews, an immersive experience in personal growth as he learned his way around the conservative intellectual movement at warp speed. All the skills of a nonprofit entrepreneur were in daily demand, from conference promotion and coalition-building to fundraising and publications.

And it was the right time to be pushing conservative ideas. No president since Calvin Coolidge had championed the fundamentals of freedom as Ronald Reagan set out to do. His no-nonsense approach to curbing the bureaucracy ("Government is the problem") and confronting the Soviets ("We win, they lose") fitted Shavano's agenda perfectly.

Andrews was able to roll out seminars in luxury venues from Palm Beach to Santa Barbara, headlined by luminaries from *National Review* and *Commentary*, the Heritage Foundation and American Enterprise Institute, Mont Pelerin and the Philadelphia Society. Some of those same big names sat for TV interviews with Roche on the *Counterpoint* program Shavano was invited to create for PBS. Mike Rosen, just then getting started on what was to be a stellar run in Denver talk radio, came on to help Fowler develop the project. But George's rugged, stoic mien proved ill-suited for television, and *Counterpoint* fizzled on launch.

Confronting 1984

More damaging was the fizzle with Colorado major donors, who balked at building the institute a permanent home on land donated by Keystone ski resort. That forced George Roche, already under heavy pressure from home-front skeptics at Hillsdale, to decree that Shavano's future, if any, must now be in Michigan, not the Rockies — but that story properly belongs in our next chapter, the decade after 1984.

The fraught year of 1984 itself dawned on an American vista of reassuring familiarity, in no way resembling the grim dystopia George Orwell had depicted in his 1949 novel of that name when John Andrews was a small boy. The specter of mankind's enslavement under totalitarian Marxism seemed to be receding, not advancing, as Reagan in the United States linked arms with Margaret Thatcher in Britain and John Paul II in the Vatican to face down the USSR.

Andrews felt encouraged about the prospects for freedom's survival, and fortunate to be helping fight that good fight. Yet there were times when he couldn't help wondering if the deep undercurrent of entropy in human affairs — what theologians call the sin problem, the Fall — might not in the end doom all the conservative movement's best efforts.

There was no denying the relentless leftward drift of public attitudes and institutions, undiminished by the superficial back-and-forth of election results. There was sad truth in the lament of some of his friends that the Right had redefined "winning" to mean merely "losing more slowly" — as the Left laughed all the way to the bank.

The Gipper was scarcely sworn in when impatient hardliners began finding fault and grousing, "Let Reagan be Reagan" — brushing aside counsels of reaching to the political center to sustain a governing coalition. George Roche, on the other hand, would often sound a cautionary note to dampen giddy expectations for how sharp a right turn could realistically be expected. He had no illusions about either the art of the possible or the corruption of power.

Credo

Sometimes upon a moody midnight John Andrews would muse about all this. But he usually managed to strike a middle course between high hopes and low spirits. He clung to a simple, sturdy credo and preached it to his comrades-in-arms: *The battle is its own reward.*

If freedom's cause could make dramatic gains, consolidate them, and gather for the next forward thrust, great—so much the better. But if bitter fighting could do no more than hold ground, or must even yield yard by yard to fierce attackers, there was no dishonor in that either—and certainly no despair. What mattered was to stay in the fight.

Because what other option did you really have? The liberties that had taken centuries to lose would take centuries to regain, if ever. The outcome of so long a struggle was, for now, unseen beyond history's horizon. On any given day, a man could either *experience* events supine and sheeplike, or *influence* events erect and unbowed, answerable only to his Lord for what use he had made of the short span of years allotted him.

For Andrews this was no hard choice. It seemed to him George Washington had put it best: "Let us raise a standard to which the wise and honest can repair. The event is in the hands of God."

Those were stirring days. America and the world were on notice there was a new sheriff, with bold moves by Reagan such as breaking the air traffic controllers' strike and going into Grenada to thwart a communist takeover. Shavano in its leadership seminars and Hillsdale in its politically incorrect classrooms were doing their small part in that wave of change.

This was more than enough to keep John leaning in. Accompanying Roche to a free-market conference in Berlin, he got to shake hands with the great Friedrich Hayek, renowned author of *The Road to Serfdom*. It was exactly ten years after his problematic handshake with Leonid Brezhnev in Moscow. The times, indeed, were a-changing.

VITAL SIGNS, 1980

The purchasing power of a dollar in your paycheck or pension fund or savings account had been more than cut in half during the decade before 1980 (table, fourth column). That's bound to put voters in a sour mood, even with continued gains in overall real income. The "Whip Inflation Now" hype during Gerald Ford's brief presidency had gone nowhere, and Jimmy Carter's weak leadership was no better. The stage was set for a Reagan landslide.

Though little noticed at the time, there were ominous storm clouds for America in the plummeting birth rate. Abortion had been the law of the land since 1973. Babies were out of fashion and feminism was in. Anything below 2.1 children meant population decline — unless offset by immigration — and here was the USA at below 1.8.

The civilizational entropy that worried John Andrews as a student of history seemed more and more real.

	1950	1960	1970	1980	1990	2000	2010	2020
Per Capita GDP (a)	$15,559	$19,614	$25,973	$32,377	$40,361	$49,911	$53,683	$62,333
Inflation	$1.00	$1.23	$1.61	$3.42	$5.43	$7.16	$9.06	$10.75
National Debt (b)	76%	43%	35%	31%	52%	55%	87%	126%
Defense Spending (b)	5.0%	9.0%	8%	5.1%	5.6%	3.1%	4.9%	3.7%
Life Expectancy	68	70	71	74	75	77	78	79
Birth Rate (c)	3.15	3.44	2.38	1.79	1.96	2.01	1.98	1.78
Born to Unwed Mothers	5%	7%	13%	21%	26%	33%	41%	41%
Born Outside USA	7%	5%	4%	6%	8%	11%	13%	14%
High School Completion	34%	40%	48%	63%	70%	83%	86%	90%
Church Attendance (d)	39%	49%	40%	40%	40%	42%	38%	31%

a) Constant 2017 dollars; b) Percent of GDP; c) Per woman lifetime; d) At least weekly

CHAPTER FIVE
REAGAN TO BUSH TO CLINTON

May 1984 – April 1994

Skinning a Knee

JOHN
ANDREWS
FOR
GOVERNOR

Paid for by Comm. to Elect John
Andrews Gov. Penn Pfiffner-Treas.

The yard signs, like everything else on the Andrews 1990
campaign, were low-budget

For him to have gotten nearly 40 percent, when the yellow-dog Republican vote was only 35 percent — heck, there was no disgrace in that. It was an achievement, him being a rookie candidate and all, running against a bullet-proof incumbent. His head knew that perfectly well, but his heart wasn't buying it. John Andrews was having a hard time coming to terms with his thumping defeat in the 1990 election for governor of Colorado.

"Think about it, man," his campaign manager said. "Three hundred thousand people showed up on Tuesday and voted for you to lead this state. You! Who else do you know that can say that? Nobody." Andrews kept trying to see it that way; couldn't make himself. It felt too much like the pathetic "moral victory" rationalizations his overmatched high school football teams used to tell themselves. Too much like the quack doctor claiming the operation was a success but the patient died. BS, all of it.

His tangle of unprocessed emotions about the lopsided loss to Gov. Roy Romer would just be a while getting sorted out, like Lincoln's story of the boy who skinned his knee and remarked it hurt too much to laugh, but he was too old to cry. The laughs, if any, were for later.

What's a Think Tank?

At least he had his feisty little think tank to go back to, now that his feisty little bid for high office had run its course. John had established the Independence Institute in Golden, Colorado, in partnership with his wife's brother, David D'Evelyn, in 1985 after the Shavano Institute moved back to Michigan.

President Reagan's triumphal year of "Morning in America," culminating in his big reelection victory in November 1984, turned out to be Shavano's peak year. That marketplace of ideas conservatives love to talk about was signaling a firm "No, thanks" in terms of event attendance, TV viewership, and donor support.

George Roche broke the news to John Andrews on May 1st, his 41st birthday. Andrews could keep his job, but it meant relocating to Hillsdale. He politely declined and by June 1st the institute had sprung back to life with a new, clearer mission targeting state policy issues and a new name evoking the Declaration of Independence.

With power devolving from Washington to the states under Reagan, policy shops in a sort of "baby Heritage Foundation" mold were popping up across the land, initially unknown to each other. Independence Institute soon became aware of kindred endeavors in Illinois, South Carolina, and Washington State, a roster that would grow rapidly as the '80s rolled on.

John still found the fundraising a hard slog, and his kids twitted him about the awkwardness of having to explain at school what on earth it could mean that "My dad runs a think tank." But he mightily loved the work, and there was sweet satisfaction in every slight move of the needle with legislators, local government officials, and the media when the institute's recommendations got noticed. He was his own boss for the first time ever, and it suited him.

The two Democrats who occupied the governor's chair in those years, the visionary Dick Lamm at first, and after 1986 his successor, the combative Roy Romer, became Andrews' foils for cheeky thought-experiments on better ways for Coloradans to govern themselves. When Lamm's frowning

Malthusian pessimism earned him the nickname "Governor Gloom," Independence Institute rolled out a rising-tide policy agenda suitable for an imaginary "Governor Growth."

When Sen. Bill Armstrong, who had breezed to reelection in 1984, urged the institute to show how liberty and limited government could equally benefit blacks, whites, and Hispanics, Andrews and D'Evelyn forged an interracial leadership alliance, the Colorado Opportunity Network, to help get that message out. Independence also worked with Tom Tancredo, a Reagan appointee in the U.S. Department of Education, to promote educational freedom. And they took on the leftist zealots seeking to weaponize environmental and energy issues.

John bagged a spot doing commentary on public radio, and wrapped some of his pieces with some by Mike Rosen, now an Independence trustee, into a book-length collection they titled *Return of the Radio Conservatives.* He found time to write and publish another little book about encountering Jesus in the Christian Science hymnal, and to travel abroad on study trips to South Korea in 1987 and the Soviet Union in 1989. Armstrong even got him a Reagan appointment to a sleepy bureaucratic backwater called the Intergovernmental Advisory Council on Education.

Double Dare

As 1989 ended, Independence Institute hosted forums to vet potential Republican gubernatorial candidates for the following year. Andrews was concerned to find the field thin and the contenders hesitant. He spent New Year's Day at his desk trying to draft a campaign brochure for some kind of 1990 run on his own part. Month by month, no one else stepped forward to challenge Romer. The candidacies of two younger friends, Tex Lezar for Attorney General of Texas and Clark Durant for U.S. Senator from Michigan, ate at John like a double-dog dare.

Finally in early April he gave an exclusive to Peter Blake of the *Rocky Mountain News*: Andrews was announcing for Lieutenant Governor. The phone blew up, but not quite in the way John had expected. Rick Grice, a pal from the Republican breakfast club, agreed to be the campaign manager. But two others in his brain trust, former gubernatorial candidate Steve Schuck and state Sen. Terry Considine, disagreed with the Lieutenant Governor play. Why not go for the top spot, they argued, if you were going to all the trouble of running? Why shoot for an office with virtually no power even if you did win?

So it came about that on April 19, 1990, in front of an inner-city high school where most Republicans wouldn't bother to campaign, but where the Independence Institute's new-style conservativism felt right at home, Andrews for Governor launched. This was outsider politics at its purest, with a candidate who had no war chest, no organization, no name ID, and no experience running for office or serving in office, anywhere, any time, at any level. What could go wrong?

There were a scant six weeks from the day John jumped in, to the day of the GOP state convention where nominees would be chosen. He took leave from Independence, turning over the reins to policy fellow Dwight Filley, and dove into a frantic round of traveling the state and working the phones, romancing delegates wherever he could.

It worked; Phase One did, anyway. On June 1st at the convention in Denver's McNichols Sports Arena, the tally was 65% for John Andrews, 28% for former congressman Mike Strang, and 7% for libertarian gadfly Robin Heid. With just two more percentage points, Strang could have forced Andrews to a runoff in the statewide August primary — which might arguably have been a net plus in terms of readying him for the fall campaign against Romer — but Heid's quirky candidacy had thwarted that, for better or worse.

So it was on to Phase Two, the longshot bid to oust Gov. Romer, who would end up outspending Andrews by five to one. Albeit John's sepulchral November mood, seen above, was understandable enough, the 150 days of that year's general election race are better seen not as tragedy but as light comedy, Gilbert and Sullivan in cowboy hats. All the *dramatis personae* entertainingly played their parts, and the foreseeable outcome came out as foreseen.

The GOP nominee (whom we won't revert to calling the kid, though in this context it's tempting) was duly accorded a photo op and handshake with President Bush at the start of his campaign and ditto with former President Reagan at its close. Waiting for his turn in the West Wing driveway with a scrum of other governor candidates, he chatted a moment with Pete Wilson of California. John felt like a rec-league softballer meeting Mickey Mantle. His moment with Reagan, months later, felt even more so — with an added sense of unease at the Gipper's already noticeable mental fogginess.

Freshly nominated, the rookie candidate flew to DC for a White House photo op with President Bush

Punchline

On one red-letter day Congressman Jack Kemp, a longtime friend of the family, flew in to headline an Andrews event. Buoyant, warm, expansive, generous, he gave the campaign a momentary jolt of energy; but no more than momentary. Another time, the guest star was Vice President Dan Quayle. John felt, in one way, honored by the visit; but Quayle fairly or unfairly had long since become a punchline in American politics. Takes one to know one, the kid thought, glancing at himself in the mirror.

Convention delegates had given the spot Andrews almost ran for, Lieutenant Governor, to Lillian Bickel, impassioned Cajun and Vietnam POW widow. Bickel was prone to act as if she belonged at the top of the ticket, provoking the campaign staff to a mix of hilarity and aggravation. Heading that staff for a few chaotic days in June, before resigning in high dudgeon, was veteran Republican warhorse Ralph Clark. Andrews' sensible refusal to accept total robotic control from above was too much for Clark's vanity. Rick Grice, whom he had tried to fire, remained as campaign manager after all.

More absurdity developed around the TABOR amendment, a tax-limit proposal John was advocating in every stump speech. State treasurer candidate Dick Sargent, apparently also fancying himself atop the ticket, pressed Andrews to back off on TABOR: "It's costing me votes." But Colorado Springs attorney Douglas Bruce, the proposal's author, took to wheedling John publicly at every rally to push TABOR harder.

Fondly as the candidate might insist that Gordon Lightfoot's lilting "Don Quixote" was just the theme song for that zany summer and fall, a better fit on most days would have been circus music from Looney Tunes. Cue the calliope, send in the clowns.

His doomed crusade couldn't catch a break. When it appeared that Romer had shown favoritism to Silverado, a savings and loan that went bust, Andrews showily returned a donation from Neil Bush, their board member and the president's son. But before that move—politically questionable at best, with its overtones of a Republican family feud—could get traction, Iraq's invasion of Kuwait took over the headlines for much of August.

John gamely soldiered on through it all. He stole a mental health day and flew to California for the Nixon Library dedication, hoping to "make important contacts" (none eventuated) or, at the very least, tap into RN's indomitable fighting spirit (some did eventuate). Lloyd King, founder of the state's leading supermarket chain, quietly kept Donna and the kids afloat financially.

His consultants, former state senators Steve Durham and Cliff Dodge, kept up a drumfire of edgy ideas to harass the incumbent. Hank Brown, running for Senate to succeed the retiring Bill Armstrong, and Gail Norton, bidding to unseat Attorney General Duane Woodard (and both headed for victory themselves), gave the kid friendly encouragement in those long days on the trail, sometimes involving as many as eight events from 7:00 in the morning to 9:00 at night. "The battle is its own reward," the kid kept telling himself. (Sorry, I have to stop calling him that.)

Never Close

It was never close. It was never even close to being close. Andrews licked his wounds and went back to running the feisty little think tank. The consolation prizes he had hoped Independence might realize from his political foray, better clout for its ideas and bigger checks from donors, weren't immediately forthcoming. But the groundbreaking ballot issues he had championed both ran well, with term limits passing and tax limits missing by a whisker—and that felt good.

The political parade fascinated him as much as ever. He met Arkansas Gov. Bill Clinton at a Democratic breakfast in Denver in mid-1991, and Hillary Clinton at a Washington event for the Intergovernmental Advisory Council on Education, of which he had now become chairman, thanks to the Bush White House. His bid for a sub-Cabinet post in the Education Department itself went nowhere, however. Obviously that dumb stunt with Neil Bush and Silverado Savings was not forgotten. "Good thing they don't know I voted for Ron Paul, the Libertarian presidential candidate, over George Bush in 1988," John reflected.

When Colorado Republicans held auditions for a 1992 challenger to Democratic Sen. Tim Wirth, Andrews briefly flirted with running, but his heart wasn't in it. He couldn't subject his family to another candidacy, after the toll 1990 had taken on them. Instead he put the institute's weight behind showing how the TABOR tax limit could benefit all Coloradans, and had the satisfaction of seeing it win.

Independence was becoming a beacon for conservatives aspiring to start think tanks in dozens of other states from Indiana to Nebraska to Nevada, and John found himself playing host to would-be policy

Former President Reagan stopped through Denver in September to raise money for the Republican ticket entrepreneurs from across the map. Loosely affiliated since the mid-'80s in what they called the Madison Group, by late 1992 the tanks were ready for a formal alliance with its own staff, budget, and brand. Tom Roe, a South Carolina philanthropist and Heritage Foundation trustee, took the lead. He and Jeff Coors, a generous supporter of Andrews' endeavors since Shavano days, convened an organizing meeting in Colorado Springs, and the State Policy Network was born.

John Andrews came within five minutes of agreeing to be the new group's executive director. But it would have meant walking away from the Independence Institute, which he couldn't bring himself to do; not yet anyway. Byron Lamm, irrepressible founder of the Indiana Policy Review, took the post instead, and would prove ideally suited for it. Lamm's partner in the Indiana venture, interestingly, had been Mike Pence, later to serve as congressman, governor, and ultimately — under Donald Trump — vice president of the United States.

But all that was far in the future when Americans went to the polls in November 1992. President Bush lost a shocker to Gov. Bill Clinton. Colorado Republicans fared no better, with Andrews' friend Terry Considine falling short in his bid for the Democrat-held Senate seat. Independence and its sister think tanks across the land spruced up their nonpartisan branding and plowed ahead with such state-level issues as school choice, tort reform, and free-market environmentalism.

John Andrews was out on one of the countless road trips that such work entailed, one spring morning in 1993, when his phone rang. What then passed for a cellphone, some readers will remember, was an ungainly grey brick with spotty service and zero eye appeal. Hefting the device with his free hand, still clipping along the interstate at 75, Andrews picked up and was delighted to hear the voice of his buddy Fritz Steiger, calling on his own brick from somewhere on the tangle of freeways around San Antonio.

The Texas Public Policy Foundation, which Steiger and business tycoon Jim Leininger had established a few years back with Andrews' encouragement, needed a CEO. Could John recommend someone? Indeed he could: himself. Conservative pastures were bound to be greener, and conservative pockets deeper, in Texas than in Colorado. It was time for a new start. By June he had handed off Independence to Tom Tancredo and decamped for the Lone Star State.

Transplant

The Yankee outsider arrived eager and expectant, but he soon began to wonder if this expedition didn't have in it more of Napoleon to Moscow than Sherman to Atlanta. Like the Alamo garrison for which San Antonio is famous, Andrews from the outset was on the defensive and on borrowed time. Transplanting from a high-visibility role in the political culture of one state to that of another isn't easy, he found — especially a state as full of itself as Texas.

The newbie encountered not only friendliness and goodwill aplenty, but also unspoken rivalries and hidden agendas in profusion. A couple of the TPPF senior staff were smarting from having been passed over for the job John now held. A glamorous heiress on the trustee board seemed to have romantic designs on him. And several members of the advisory board were jockeying to use the foundation as a launch pad to public office.

These included George W. Bush, son of the former president, and Rob Mosbacher, son of the former Secretary of Commerce, both looking at the 1994 race for governor, and Harold "Tex" Lezar, Andrews' old office mate in White House speechwriting and unsuccessful 1990 candidate for Attorney General, who had his eye on Lieutenant Governor in 1994. Wherever John went, jetting around the vast state every week to raise money and peddle policy, the air was thick with intrigue.

When he naively sounded the trustees on moving the TPPF office from San Antonio, where founder and chairman Jim Leininger was based, to Austin, the state capital, the backlash was swift and severe. Conservatives all over Texas, come to find out, bitterly as they might distrust each other from Dallas to Houston to Midland, were as one in their suspicion and loathing of liberal Austin. The idea died quickly, and with it some of John's political capital.

When word of Lezar's intended candidacy reached Bob Bullock, Democrat incumbent in the uniquely powerful office of Lieutenant Governor (a choke point for all legislation by virtue of its control over the state Senate), the shrewd old operator called Andrews on the carpet and browbeat him mercilessly, LBJ-style. For good measure, Bullock then recruited the salty left-liberal columnist Molly Ivins to do a scathing hit piece on the Yankee outsider's alleged misdeeds in Colorado and nefarious intentions for Texas. It left John's ears ringing like nothing he could remember since getting his bell rung in freshman football, long long ago.

Mixed in with all the madness there were plenty of rollicking good times and the occasional political adrenaline rush. Mike Watson, the good ol' boy Aggie who was

Andrews' right hand at TPPF, saw to that. John might be rubbing elbows one day with Sen. Phil Gramm, the next with former Gov. Bill Clements, and the next with San Antonio Spurs star David Robinson — dubbed "The Admiral" for his Naval Academy pedigree.

Foundation chairman Jim Leininger rose in John's estimation when he coolly sent the brash George W. Bush away empty-handed after hearing the gubernatorial hopeful's fundraising pitch. Bush, of course, would go on to win Leininger's support, capture the GOP nomination, defeat incumbent Gov. Ann Richards, and forge a productive bipartisan alliance with Lt. Gov. Bullock — who easily won reelection against Lezar.

Not Me, Us

All sorts of Texas fun. Increasingly, though, as 1994 drew on, on lonely evenings in his drab little apartment, Andrews kept hearing the echo of something his first submarine skipper, Bob Gavazzi, loved to say: "If it doesn't feel good, you're not doing it right." The ribald wisecrack, he saw, made a serious point. Maybe the Yankee outsider was never going to find his way inside. Maybe he should quit trying to make water run uphill. Maybe enough was enough.

Hadn't there been something escapist about this Texas move from the start? Donna gamely flew down for a house-hunting weekend in Austin (evil Austin!) but she had her hands full in Denver, with both of their daughters going through deep waters personally, and with Dave D'Evelyn, Donna's brother, having died in a tragic plane crash. Out for a run on a spring morning in San Antonio, John had an epiphany. His preoccupation with goals for "my life" was all wrong. He needed to start focusing on "our life."

So it was that in late April, after not quite one year at the Texas Public Policy Foundation, John Andrews rejoined his family in Colorado. On May 1st, Donna threw a surprise party for his 50th birthday, and another grateful decade went into the books.

Grateful, yes — but marred with self-indulgence. The lark of running for governor on a whim, soon followed by the lark of bolting off to Texas — "lighting out for the territory," as Huck Finn called it — these hadn't been his finest hours. His family had paid a price for them.

All painfully true. Yet he had set both the Independence Institute and the State Policy Network on their feet, and had seen TABOR into the state constitution, and had parted amicably from TPPF with lessons learned. Oh yes, at Easter 1993 he had also become a baptized Christian. And now, home had never looked sweeter. Really, how could the next decade top this one?

VITAL SIGNS, 1990

Growth in real per capita income was still clipping along at a happy 25 percent per decade (table, fifth column), despite the nation having weathered a financial crash and energy bust in the late 1980s. Andrews knew it all too well, having stood by as a stage prop while Gov. Romer claimed credit for Colorado's share of the economic rebound in his easy 1990 win.

Demographics were still trending unfavorably, however. Birth rates were up a little, but still below the 2.1 replacement level. Illegitimate births now accounted for more than one in four children nationally, with all the woes of fatherlessness and poverty sure to follow in their train.

The proportion of foreign-born in U.S. census data had doubled in two decades. Though arguably helpful to America's labor force and tax base, it was a trend with profound cultural consequences in the years ahead. John knew he'd be a grandfather before long. Would his son's son grow up in a country even remotely resembling the vanished USA of Davy Crockett and "I Like Ike"?

	1950	1960	1970	1980	1990	2000	2010	2020
Per Capita GDP (a)	$15,559	$19,614	$25,973	$32,377	$40,361	$49,911	$53,683	$62,333
Inflation	$1.00	$1.23	$1.61	$3.42	$5.43	$7.16	$9.06	$10.75
National Debt (b)	76%	43%	35%	31%	52%	55%	87%	126%
Defense Spending (b)	5.0%	9.0%	8%	5.1%	5.6%	3.1%	4.9%	3.7%
Life Expectancy	68	70	71	74	75	77	78	79
Birth Rate (c)	3.15	3.44	2.38	1.79	1.96	2.01	1.98	1.78
Born to Unwed Mothers	5%	7%	13%	21%	26%	33%	41%	41%
Born Outside USA	7%	5%	4%	6%	8%	11%	13%	14%
High School Completion	34%	40%	48%	63%	70%	83%	86%	90%
Church Attendance (d)	39%	49%	40%	40%	40%	42%	38%	31%

a) Constant 2017 dollars
b) Percent of GDP
c) Per woman lifetime
d) At least weekly

CHAPTER SIX
CLINTON TO BUSH

May 1994 – April 2004

The Accidental Senator

Could free airtime for presidential candidates check the
spiraling cost of campaigns?
Andrews and TCI Cable News undertook to find out with
Race for the Presidency

For the first few days, everyone calling him "Senator" was like sweet music in his ears. But inside a week he caught on: *It mostly just means they want something from me. There's always an agenda.*

It was January 1999 and John Andrews found himself, almost by accident, a member of the Colorado Senate. Andrews had been soldiering along in a less-than-ideal job the previous summer, feeling somewhat stalled, when Mike Coffman, senator from their reliably Republican suburb at the time, suggested he seek to fill the vacancy that would result if Coffman won his race for State Treasurer.

Mike did prevail in November 1998, riding a GOP tide that also saw Bill Owens elected governor, and a month later John prevailed over five other contenders in the vacancy committee. Now here he was, a rookie lawmaker delightedly learning to play the legislative game — and tune out the flattery.

Skunk Works

Here indeed was a turn of events never foreseen by the chastened interloper skulking home to Colorado from Texas in 1994. It had felt great then, just being back, but there was the question of what to do with himself, how to make a living. The Colorado political parade, for the moment at least, had pretty much passed him by.

Oilman Bruce Benson, who had been Republican state chairman when Andrews took on Roy Romer in 1990, was on track to be the gubernatorial nominee this time, and would eventually lose by about the same margin while spending ten times what John had spent. There were early signs of the national GOP sweep that would capture Congress for the first time in 40 years, but Colorado wouldn't figure in that triumph. Independence Institute was thriving under Tom Tancredo's leadership, and John toyed with creating a "chair in constitutional government" over there for himself — only to scrap the idea after a week or two. It felt forced.

What did seem to have possibilities was television. Maybe the short-lived *Counterpoint* TV series of a few years ago could be made to fly after all. America's cable industry was centered in Denver, and one of its pioneers, John Saeman, had been a benefactor to Andrews' past efforts in policy and politics. Saeman now brokered an introduction to the legendary Bob Magness, whose Tele-Communications Inc. (TCI) was the largest cable operator in the country — and TCI Cable News was born.

Initially the venture bore no such grand title, of course. Andrews was allowed a cubicle, an expense account, the Magness name to conjure with, and turned loose as a one-man skunk works to develop conservative programming, which was vanishingly scarce in the broadcast-dominated TV marketplace of those days. Serendipity connected him with Bob Chitester of Erie, Pennsylvania, famed within PBS as the creator of Milton Friedman's phenomenally successful series, *Free to Choose*. John came to esteem Bob almost like an older brother, and they forged a fertile partnership.

After some trial and error, they settled on an issues-and-interview show concept set in an imaginary small-town eatery, the Damn Right Diner. The host would be David Asman, an affable young reporter at the *Wall Street Journal*. The featured issue for their *Damn Right* pilot was term limits, with Arkansas Governor Mike Huckabee as guest star. So far, so good. Production began and spirits were high. The show was cheeky and fun. It popped with energy. It worked; they thought so anyway.

But who would air the show, who would sponsor it, and would anyone watch? That was a tougher nut to crack. TCI with its 18 million cable subscribers seemed an attractive core audience, but the impressive company Magness had built existed up to that time solely as a carrier, not a programmer. Habits run deep. A corporate culture doesn't change overnight just because some political protégé of the boss snaps his fingers.

John Malone, Magness' likely successor, did believe in diversifying the company into content, and was strongly libertarian-minded to boot; Andrews in fact helped him get a seat on the Cato Institute board. But Bob Thompson, Peter Barton, and others in senior management, Democrats to a man, never warmed up to "Damn Right." The skunk works was in bad odor, as far as they were concerned.

In the end, what sank the project was Fox News bursting on the scene in late 1996 with the muscle of Rupert Murdoch and the savvy of Roger Ailes behind it. Malone, taking charge after Magness was felled by cancer just at that time, reasonably decided to cede the field to Fox.

One Bubble Away

For John Andrews, though, merely in his avocation as a spectator at the parade, what a ride it had been. Dining with Rush Limbaugh in New York and with Milton Friedman in Santa Rosa. Dickering with movie mogul Barry Diller in Hollywood and with CNN kingfish Ted Turner (and his wife, Jane Fonda) in Atlanta.

Poking around Little Rock with Mike Huckabee on what the governor laughingly called "the Clinton scandal tour." Huddling with Jack Kemp just after the Dole-Kemp '96 GOP ticket was nominated to take on Clinton-Gore. Lining up various challengers to President Clinton for appearances on TCI's free-airtime experiment, *Race for the Presidency*. And so many other great moments.

Was TCI Cable News a near miss, a hairsbreadth from success? Hardly. But John liked to console himself by relating a little parable about persistence his father sometimes told. Before 7-Up became a world-famous brand and made its inventor a fortune, the story went, another soft-drink experimenter concocted a lemon-lime blend with bubbles in its logo. He brought to market first 1-Up, then 2-Up, then 3-Up, but none of them caught on. Undaunted, he tried again with 4-Up, then 5-Up, then 6-Up — at that point finally folding, without ever realizing how close he had been to greatness. *Just one bubble away, one more bubble,* John Andrews and Bob Chitester ruefully told each other.

Sardonic humor at his own expense was a handy coping mechanism, John found. He'd often say of his 1990 race: *I was almost elected governor; almost. All we needed was another million dollars or another million votes.* The moral-victory mentality died hard, it seemed, for a guy raised on Principia's perennial athletic futility against Burroughs or Country Day. Down the years, though, he took quiet satisfaction in glimpsing such accomplished newsmen as David Asman on Fox or Jonathan Karl on ABC and knowing it had been TCI that got them their first break in television.

The fat lady officially sang for John Andrews' television career on an April day in 1997 when he was fired from Tele-Communications Inc. on zero notice by John Malone's new henchman Leo Hindery, who had arrived from San Francisco professing Republican beliefs but soon proved to be all-in for Bill Clinton.

Building Character

Walking out into a spring snowstorm after undergoing the classic, cold cutoff corporate ritual — here's a box, empty your desk, turn in your badge, be out of the building by 5:00, and don't come back — Andrews gritted his teeth and tried to be philosophical: *They say this builds character, and I hope so. Because it sure doesn't build self-esteem.*

Self-esteem is vastly overrated, however, and in his best moments John knew that. Something would turn up, he told himself, and sure enough, something did. Former Attorney General Edwin Meese, one of Ronald Reagan's most trusted lieutenants, had come to know John Andrews slightly through the Heritage Foundation. He was helping Jack Singlaub, a retired Army general and right-wing firebrand, stand up a new, proposed cable channel called American National Network. They needed an organizer and rainmaker to bring ANN from concept to reality. Might Andrews be their man?

Months of farce ensued, where each of the three, along with a sharp-dealing Hollywood promoter named Michael Leighton, looked to the others for the magic fuel that would give their leaden concept liftoff. Their unreadiness for prime time was epic. Their good intentions paved, if not the road to hell, certainly the road to helplessness. Tempers frayed, mistrust flared, messy litigation loomed. By summer's end, John Andrews felt lucky to escape the collapsing project in one piece.

He landed on his feet as vice president of development at Greater Europe Mission, a Colorado-based ministry bringing the New Testament to old Europe. To keep his hand in politically, he recruited civil-rights lawyer Dani

Newsum as a sparring partner and began doing a daily mini-debate called *Bad News* for Colorado Public Television. Later renamed *Head On* and with Susan Barnes-Gelt taking Newsum's place, it would run for another dozen years.

Nineteen ninety-eight left its mark as a year of tempest and upheaval. Though awestruck by the devotion of the missionaries he was getting to know at GEM, Andrews couldn't find his footing in the new job. Assigned to edit the manuscript for a forthcoming 50th-anniversary history of the organization, whose founder, Bob Evans, had been close to Billy Graham, he was invited to ghostwrite Graham's foreword to the book. A signal honor, he reflected, given that the beloved evangelist would probably be remembered when Nixon and other U.S. presidents were forgotten.

Still John was awash in distractions and guiltily knew he wasn't giving full value to his boss at GEM, the aptly-named Ted Noble. There was the sudden death of his father, then the sudden death of a favorite aunt, Congressman Hutchinson's widow, then the worsening signs of dementia in Donna's mother, then the wedding of his son. And his own marriage was once again in extremis, with only himself to blame, as before.

By autumn the storms had subsided, however, the missions job was history, and out of the clearing skies like a bolt from the blue came this opportunity in Senate District 27. John Andrews was left pinching himself as Christmas neared.

Counting to 18

At that time, turning the page into 1999, five million Coloradans relied on one hundred elected representatives to make and maintain their laws. There were 35 seats in the state Senate and 65 in the state House. Hence what was sometimes called the 18-33-1 "combination lock" for passage of a bill into law: a majority of yes-votes in each chamber plus one signature from the governor.

Colorado's constitution gave the General Assembly just 120 real days in each calendar year to do all its business — or as some would say, all its damage — which meant a stiff pace and no dawdling, with upward of 700 items proposed for enactment and clamoring for legislators' attention.

Senator Andrews, the eager freshman from Arapahoe County, had lived long enough to know that politics is downstream from culture, that a nation's songs precede its laws, and all the rest of it. Still he couldn't entirely resist the initial rush that came with a prestigious title and a share of official power. It was a trip, no two ways about it.

Soon enough, though, sitting under a Judiciary Committee chairwoman far more liberal than himself and under an Education Committee chairman far less showy than himself — albeit both were his fellow Republicans, respected elders in the twenty-member majority caucus — John began to see how hard it might often be to count 18 votes on the floor.

The legislative day, he quickly realized, was largely given over to grinding work, leaving precious little time for political posturing. But Andrews took to the new challenge as if born to it. The splendid old Capitol itself had an atmosphere of solemnity and seriousness that seemed to call forth the best from everyone serving there.

Built in the 1890s, its architect had been the great Elijah Myers, who also designed — John learned with mild astonishment — the Texas State Capitol where Lt. Gov. Bob

Bullock had theatrically woodshedded him a few years ago *and* the Michigan State Capitol where Gov. Mennen Williams had kindly welcomed him a lifetime ago. Mark Twain was right, the rookie reflected: sometimes history does rhyme.

For an office mate, he drew Mark Hillman, an impressive young wheat farmer from Colorado's eastern plains. They became fast friends and staunch conservative allies. John's assigned seat in the Senate chamber was in the front row between Sen. Marilyn Musgrave of Fort Morgan and Sen. Jim Congrove of Arvada, two of the body's strongest advocates for liberty and limited government. Andrews had scarcely been there a week before they started urging him to run for leadership; he scoffed.

Commandments

Colorado conservatives were feeling their strength that winter. Bill Owens was settling in as the state's first Republican governor in a quarter-century. Tom Tancredo was unsettling everyone in sight as a new member of Congress — the first alumnus of a State Policy Network think tank to make the jump to national office. Owens was nettled when Andrews joined forces with Democratic Sen. Ed Perlmutter to insist the governor's highway bonds go to a vote of the people as constitutionally required, but the annoyance soon blew over (and in due course the bond issue passed easily).

The searing moment of that 1999 legislative session came on an April afternoon when a routine hearing of Sen. Dottie Wham's judiciary committee, with Perlmutter and Andrews in attendance, was interrupted by the horrific news of a mass shooting at Columbine High School. A new era of random violence in American life had begun.

Then suddenly it was mid-May and John got his first taste of how spring fever can sweep over a hundred lawmakers in the hectic final days of a session. Jim Congrove, a salty ex-cop with a mischievous streak, seized on the "school's out" mood to enlist his fellow Republicans in a scheme to force adjournment two hours early on the last evening, leaving a crowded calendar of low-priority bills unaddressed. The pranksters ultimately relented, but the merriment was lost on Senate President Ray Powers.

As summer came on, John Andrews was approached by his friend Bruce Cairns, a leading Christian conservative in Denver's south suburbs. Shock waves from the Columbine massacre were still reverberating in the state. Might this tragedy be an opportunity, Cairns asked, to reassert America's foundational understanding of right and wrong in the public square?

Andrews quickly seized on the idea, announcing his intention to propose a bill in the 2000 session requiring display of the Ten Commandments in all public-school classrooms and public buildings. There was the predictable howl and hand-wringing from the atheist Left, of course, but less-vocal support from the ostensibly God-fearing Right than he might have hoped for.

Joining a US-Canada evangelism team for a short-term mission in Cambodia later that year, where he was honored to speak on God and government at a convocation of high-ranking government leaders, John mused that his own truest "mission call" for such matters was probably much closer to home.

The year 2000 shaped up as a big one politically. George W. Bush would try to take back the White House for Republicans. John Andrews had been reintroduced to "W" when Gov. Bill Owens, always close to the Bush family, had brought the Texas governor in for a campaign stop.

Andrews himself must face the voters in November, his Senate predecessor's unexpired term having run its course. Additionally, in a textbook case of counting unhatched chickens, he began quietly lining up votes within the GOP caucus to become majority leader after the fall election. Think of it: majority leader!

Hot Potato

But first there were 120 days of legislating to be gotten through, and along with John's bills on school reform, election reform, and the like, there was this year's hot potato, the Ten Commandments bill. It wasn't logical that alarms should be sounded over reminding Colorado schoolchildren of an ancient and venerated law code already proclaimed on the walls of the U.S. Supreme Court chamber and on a marble monument in the State Capitol's own front yard; but sounded they were.

Some Republicans feared the political consequences of having to cast a recorded vote on the bill. President Powers and other heavyweights entreated Andrews to drop the whole thing. He politely declined. Lacking Sen. Wham's vote, however, he would be unable even to get the measure out of committee. Under the circumstances, why fight on?

Up stepped Democratic Sen. Stan Matsunaka just then and — beware Greeks bearing gifts — generously offered his vote to keep the bill alive for floor debate. Clearly the Dems were already drafting their "theocracy bogeyman" ad campaign to target swing districts next fall.

It grieved John to realize that America was now so far gone that "Thou shalt not kill" could become a wedge issue in elections. But that being so, should he go ahead and immolate himself on the issue, or should he pull back, spare his vulnerable or vacillating colleagues, and live to fight another day?

In a brief speech on the Senate floor, he withdrew the bill, a vote not yet having been called. There was far more of symbolism than of substance in the proposal after all, he knew. The self-governance of a free people is a long game, a marathon, not a sprint. That too he knew.

"Backbone" was Sen. Andrews' rallying cry as he ran for another term in 2000

In November 2000 Bruce Cairns was elected to the state Senate from Aurora. By that time Andrews had done another summer mission trip, this time to Cuba; his election campaign, managed by Wil Armstrong, son of the former U.S. senator, had succeeded; and his vote-counting for leadership, managed by attorney David Balmer, a former North Carolina legislator, had succeeded too, after a fashion.

But only after a fashion — for Democrats had flipped three Republican seats and taken the Senate for the first time in 40 years. It would only be a 17-member GOP *minority* that was left for Sen. Andrews to lead, come January. In the grand scheme of things, though, power changing hands in one of 99 state legislative chambers mattered little in comparison to that year's supreme political prize, the presidency.

Would Al Gore and the Democrats or George W. Bush and the Republicans lead the United States of America for the next four years? That race wasn't decided on November

7, Election Day, or in the next week, or even in the next month. Not until December 12 were Florida's 25 electoral votes awarded to Bush by a decision of the U.S. Supreme Court, breaking the deadlock.

The ruling came on a morning when, purely by chance, Sen. John Andrews and his family happened to be outside the court building enroute to a tour of the United States Capitol, arranged for them by Congressman Tom Tancredo. Tina, Jennifer, and Daniel had not been to the nation's capital since their father broke with Nixon and moved west when they were tiny. John and Donna wanted to show them historic sites and shrines from Washington to Williamsburg at this first Christmas season of the new millennium.

The verdict in *Bush v. Gore* put an exclamation point on the significance and resilience of those American institutions Andrews had dedicated his life to serving. Seldom had the political parade seemed more vibrantly alive and dramatic to him.

Into the Minority

Back in Colorado, under the Gold Dome, the parade had its own vivid color and cadence even if history wasn't watching on tiptoe. Senate Republicans had held the majority since before Sen. Mark Hillman was born. But now the people had spoken, and that majestic ceremonial of American self-government, the peaceful transfer of power, was once again enacted. The GOP would take a back seat for now, Hillman would become Andrews' wingman as assistant minority leader, and Democrats would take the gavel.

The state's proud heritage as a melting pot of many nationalities was affirmed in the new president, Sen. Stan

Matsunaka of Loveland, scion of indomitable Japanese immigrants, and in his majority leader, Sen. Bill Thiebaut of Pueblo, heir of the French pioneer tradition from Louisiana territorial days. John Andrews knew both as worthy adversaries, and they made an effective team—Matsunaka, quiet-spoken and shrewd, a subtle strategist, balanced by the keen and affable Thiebaut, who liked to joke that for him, as the father of ten, the Senate could hold no surprises.

Challenging his Republican caucus to battle the Democrats every day on every bill, John placed on each member's desk a countdown calendar cube marking off the 700-odd days until voters could (it was hoped) hand them back the majority.

Yet for the state at large, accustomed to divided government from a dozen years of Democratic Gov. Dick Lamm and another dozen of Gov. Roy Romer—with the legislature in Republican hands all the while—the previous two years of a more readily attainable 18-33-1 for GOP goals seemed but a fleeting anomaly as the 2001 session heated up. That which absolutely *must* get done would still get done somehow. Andrews honestly sometimes wondered if divided government wasn't actually preferable for the protection of Coloradans' life, liberty, and property.

This was now John Andrews' third year as a member of the Colorado General Assembly, and its rhythms as a part-time citizen legislature were becoming second nature to him. The 120-day annual limit for regular sessions, placed in the state constitution in 1987 by then House Majority Leader Chris Paulson (who went on to chair the Andrews for Governor campaign in 1990), stood as an important barrier to the professionalization and "congressionalization" that had turned many other legislatures into perpetual mischief machines where adjournment was unheard of and government could metastasize unchecked.

This meant that in Colorado, even for members of leadership, the General Assembly was not a full-time job. Andrews had to find other productive uses for the months of June through December, even though a legacy from his mother's family exempted him from scrambling, as some colleagues had to do, to supplement their $30,000 per annum legislative salary. Semi-official travel in the summer and fall was part of the answer for John.

One of his destinations in 2001 was Taiwan, the defiant bastion of liberty offshore from Communist China. Another was Israel, where he led the first-ever Colorado legislative delegation to visit the embattled Jewish state. That trip came just six weeks after the 9/11 Islamic terror attacks on New York and Washington, and his daughter shed apprehensive tears for her parents as she saw them off in Denver. But he argued Israel was probably safer from terrorism than any place else on earth right then, and so it proved.

Conventioneering with likeminded legislators from across the fifty states was another off-session staple. Democrats and the occasional moderate Republican flocked to gatherings of the National Conference of State Legislatures (NCSL), funded with tax dollars, where the latest ideas for bigger government were on offer. Among the GOP colleagues of John Andrews likely to turn up at NCSL events were Senators Norma Anderson of Lakewood, Dave Owen of Greeley, and Ron Teck of Grand Junction, as well as the Harvard-educated Speaker of the House, Russell George of Rifle.

Senate and House conservatives, by contrast, gravitated to the American Legislative Exchange Council (ALEC), where policy solutions aligned with liberty and limited government were hammered out. ALEC, largely reliant on private donations, was well known to Andrews from his Shavano and Independence Institute days back in the 1980s. Its issue analysis, along with that of the State Policy Network, which he had helped launch in the 1990s, proved valuable as Republicans girded to take back the Colorado Senate in 2002.

The message would be that not only were Republicans better stewards of the Constitution, but also that Democrats were out of step on common-sense values. GOP senators ran bills they knew Democrats would kill, but which would come back to haunt the party in power at election time.

Shut the door on driver's licenses or other government-issued ID for illegal aliens? Damn right, says the average voter. Provide for all schoolchildren to start the day by pledging allegiance to the flag? Damn right again. But wait, not so fast there, says the Senate Democratic majority. *Gotcha! The campaign mailer writes itself.*

What the Surgeon Said

Bill Shine of Fox News, formerly a producer with TCI Cable News, seized on the Pledge of Allegiance controversy when John Andrews called him about it. Sean Hannity had Democratic Sen. Ken Gordon on the air and punched his lights out. The Senate minority offices rang with cheers and laughter as a tape of the encounter played on a loop. GOP morale was high as the session ended and campaigning got underway.

A summer ritual for Andrews since the 1950s had been hiking up one of Colorado's many 14,000-foot peaks. This year it was fabled Long's Peak in Rocky Mountain National Park, a solid twelve hours on the trail for John and his son, Daniel, a Denver police officer. The climb was without incident, but in hobbling down the last few miles he realized a long-postponed hip replacement could no longer be put off, politics or no politics. Just before going under with the anesthetic on a morning in mid-September, he saw the surgeon lean in close and say, "I hope you and the Republicans have this election well in hand." And as it turned out, they did.

John was back on the campaign trail, crutches and all, in time for a short stint of door-to-door canvassing in Colorado Springs, where county commissioner and black conservative Ed Jones was bidding to reclaim a Democrat-held seat — and on election night, with poetic justice, it was Jones's victory that tipped the Senate back to an 18–17 GOP majority.

Republicans had swept. Gov. Bill Owens was reelected easily, bringing with him a new lieutenant governor, pro-life champion Jane Norton. U.S. Sen. Wayne Allard won a second term. Marilyn Musgrave, John Andrews' close ally in the Senate, was elected to Congress, as was state Republican chair Bob Beauprez of Boulder, who prevailed in Colorado's newly minted 7th congressional district. Unsuspected by any of them at the time, it was to be the high-water mark of Republican strength in the state, never again matched from then to now.

When legislators caucused two days later, John Andrews defeated Ron Teck for Senate president by a 10–8 margin. His choice for Majority Leader, Mark Hillman, deadlocked in a 9–9 tie with arch-moderate Norma Anderson, and a job-sharing compromise was agreed to, she holding the post in 2003, he in 2004. For Andrews, that week's events marked a gratifying turnaround from his crushing defeat for governor a dozen years ago. A headline in the *Rocky Mountain News* said it all: "Andrews Rises from Political Dead."

But the next week held something even better in store, as Daniel and Stephanie presented John and Donna with their first grandchild, Ian Michael Andrews, born Nov. 13, 2002, in Littleton. It was one of those moments that John found recurring over and over in his political life, when the elemental conservative "why" of it all was affirmed anew.

To him, the little fellow's bright eyes and angelic smile outshone all the stars in the sky. No worldly honors or titles could come close. Samuel Johnson had spoken truly, John felt: "To be happy at home is the ultimate result of all ambition." The state and all its trappings really exist for nothing else, C. S. Lewis had added, quoting this. Just so.

Young Ian, age two months, was present at the festivities when his grandfather took over as Senate president as the 2003 session began. Everyone agreed his decorum was impeccable on this first occasion to spectate at the political parade. There would be many more.

What Overton Noticed

President Andrews was ably staffed by Cliff Dodge, William Mutch, Sandy Drago, and Renee White, seasoned hands all. For the key administrative post of Secretary of the Senate, he had tapped the imperturbable and razor-sharp Mona Heustis. The post of President Pro Tem, though largely honorific, became an early flashpoint when Sen. Ken Chlouber of Leadville wrested it away from Sen. Doug Lamborn of Colorado Springs, who had the votes. Both were angling to run for Congress, and in that rivalry the phlegmatic Lamborn eventually bested the volatile Chlouber.

Ken was easily the most colorful member of the body in those days, and the most unpredictable. He secured the Pro Tem post by threatening to switch parties and restore the Senate to Democratic control. Yet impossible to be mad at, he waggishly needled John Andrews that the latter's "backbone" campaign slogan should rather be called "hambone" or "wishbone."

Chlouber as a former hardrock miner had a soft spot for labor unions, and it was his vote that killed Gov. Owens' cherished right-to-work bill. Rounding up 18 votes on what should have been sure-fire Republican bills was easier said than done. A measure outlawing racial preferences fell one vote short despite an eloquent appeal by the sponsor, Ed Jones, who was taunted with racial slurs by opponents of the bill.

Andrews fought hard to enact an Academic Bill of Rights, hated by the campus left and backed by the fiery ex-Communist David Horowitz, but skillful lobbying within the GOP ranks by timorous university presidents forced him to accept a watered-down "memorandum of understanding" on intellectual diversity, impossible to enforce.

Worse, some legislative victories were annulled by the judiciary. Such was the fate of a far-reaching school voucher bill, shepherded to passage by John's Arapahoe County colleague, Rep. Nancy Spence, and of a congressional redistricting bill pushed through in the waning hours of the 2003 session but voided by the Democrat-dominated Colorado Supreme Court and state attorney general Ken Salazar.

Writing this account twenty years later—amid headlines about the U.S. Supreme Court blocking a move by Colorado's high court to throw former President Trump off the 2024 ballot—John Andrews was struck by the predominance of legislative losses over wins in his recollection of those days. The defeats still stung, even after all this time. Yet how different as a state would Colorado actually be, he asked himself, if all the bills that didn't quite get into the statute books back then, instead had done so? His frank answer: not a lot.

Aren't all our efforts for political change, win or lose, ultimately as inconsequential as pulling your fist out of a bucket of water? Provided, that is, the parameters of change are kept within constitutional bounds? Radical change — emptying the figurative bucket altogether, or flooding it to overflow — is another matter, of course. In the early 2000s, that kind of radical reset seemed but a remote possibility. Whereas with today's bitter polarization among the states and between the parties, the formerly unthinkable seems all too thinkable now.

The Overton Window, or acceptable range of policy options at a given time within a given body politic (so named for the late Joseph Overton of Michigan's Mackinac Center, whom Andrews knew from the '80s and '90s), was shifting ever leftward throughout John's lifetime, due to progressives' long march through the institutions. Legislative changes at the margins, whether achieved or prevented, were but consequences of the shift, not causative in themselves.

Meanwhile, Andrews reflected wryly, perhaps the best summary of the ongoing scrum under the Capitol dome came from his friend Rep. Dorothy Gottlieb, one of Denver's last surviving Republican officeholders. "The trouble with having a hundred people called legislators gathered here for months on end," she liked to say, "is that they all feel compelled to legislate." Everyone, that is, thinks they have to justify his or her own existence, and when seen from the remove of a decade or two, the net result is usually not all that momentous.

For which, thank goodness, the Senate president told himself as the sand ran rapidly through the hourglass on his two sessions of glory, 2003 and 2004. His heartland conservative instincts, bred in the bone, told him that as it was with throwing the football (*pace* Woody Hayes), so it was with letting loose lawmakers: more bad things than good things can happen. Be glad you don't get all the government you pay for, we're told. John Andrews was.

VITAL SIGNS, 2000

With the Cold War finally behind them, Americans had leisure to toy with cockeyed theories like "the end of history," gossip about morsels like the stained blue dress, and fret over whether Y2K would fry all the world's computers.

Defense spending as a share of GDP (table, 3rd column from right) was by far the lowest in John Andrews' lifetime — but more than ample to handle minor conflicts in faraway places like Somalia and Bosnia, plus the occasional terrorist pinprick. The peace dividend seemed to have sapped fiscal discipline more than stiffening it, however. Federal debt as a share of GDP continued steadily rising, after hitting a low in the 1980s. Nothing occurring nationally or internationally at the turn of the millennium, though, was compelling enough to divert much of Andrews' attention from the Colorado homefront issues then absorbing him. The holiday from history would be over sooner than any of them knew.

	1950	1960	1970	1980	1990	2000	2010	2020
Per Capita GDP (a)	$15,559	$19,614	$25,973	$32,377	$40,361	$49,911	$53,683	$62,333
Inflation	$1.00	$1.23	$1.61	$3.42	$5.43	$7.16	$9.06	$10.75
National Debt (b)	76%	43%	35%	31%	52%	55%	87%	126%
Defense Spending (b)	5.0%	9.0%	8%	5.1%	5.6%	3.1%	4.9%	3.7%
Life Expectancy	68	70	71	74	75	77	78	79
Birth Rate (c)	3.15	3.44	2.38	1.79	1.96	2.01	1.98	1.78
Born to Unwed Mothers	5%	7%	13%	21%	26%	33%	41%	41%
Born Outside USA	7%	5%	4%	6%	8%	11%	13%	14%
High School Completion	34%	40%	48%	63%	70%	83%	86%	90%
Church Attendance (d)	39%	49%	40%	40%	40%	42%	38%	31%

a) Constant 2017 dollars; b) Percent of GDP; c) Per woman lifetime; d) At least weekly

CHAPTER SEVEN
BUSH TO OBAMA

May 2004 – April 2014

Flogging a Book

Growing by the year, the Western Conservative Summit put Colorado
Christian University on the map nationally

If "flogging his book," as they called it, was what an author had to do to generate sales, okay, he'd do it. But there was something groveling and grubby about the whole process, John Andrews felt. It was a summer day in 2011. He stood blinking in the sun-glare on Sixth Avenue in New York, taking stock of how it had gone with his three minutes on the Fox News morning show with fellow Coloradan Jon Scott.

Were viewers across the country rushing out (or logging on) at this very moment to get their own copy of *Responsibility Reborn: A Citizen's Guide to the Next American Century*? One could always hope so, but Andrews doubted he had said anything compelling enough in that quick interview to set off a stampede to the bookstores.

"So for this," he told himself with a philosophic shrug, turning north toward his hotel on Central Park, "you flew all the way out here from Denver." Time for some phone interviews with small-market talk radio here and there across the country, then out to LaGuardia to catch his flight home.

Responsibility Reborn was the book John had been promising himself to write for who knows how long. He'd gone into hiding for six months in 2008 and finally banged the darn thing out. Another couple of years finding a publisher—of sorts—and now here it was at last, bursting upon a waiting world.

Andrews had long been concerned that conservatives tended to pay all their attention to individual freedom, with little thought for freedom's price and condition, the other side of the coin, personal responsibility. The book was meant as a corrective to that.

And really—as he told interviewers over and over—it was three books in one: a love letter to America and what makes her special; an account of his lessons learned from a long life in politics; and a reflection on how the nation can find its way forward in responsible freedom.

Andrews was under no illusion that it possessed either the brio of an overnight bestseller or the stubborn staying power of a cult classic. But it was his stab at a testament of truth, and he felt better for having finally spelled it out and sent it forth, come what may. It was to him as the discharging of a debt, something he owed to the political heroes depicted on the book's cover: the likes of Jefferson, Tocqueville, Lincoln, Coolidge, Goldwater, Nixon, Solzhenitsyn, and Reagan.

In the Mirror

The responsibility book may never have gotten written if Andrews had played his cards a bit differently several years earlier. Change the political landscape just slightly, and a longer tenure in the state Senate, or even a move to the U.S. House, could arguably have been his. To the end of his days, however, John would say he never regretted the decisions he'd made.

Six years and out for his senatorial service were locked in when he chose to be sworn in on Dec. 30, 1998, instead of two weeks later when the new General Assembly would already be underway. Gaming the term-limits measure he had helped to place in the state constitution back in 1990 just struck him as a cheap trick. "Live under the laws that you make" was one of his personal-responsibility axioms, after all.

As for a possible path to Congress, term limits played into that scenario as well. His friend Tom Tancredo had promised to self-limit at six years when winning his first congressional race in 1998 — but by early 2004 he had succumbed to the

"America needs me" siren song and declared his self-limit inoperative. Meeting with Andrews, he appealed for the Senate president to be an endorser, not a challenger, in Tom's upcoming race.

Time was, John very much pictured himself in the role of congressman, but that impulse had by now spent itself in him. "Don't worry yourself on my account," he told Tancredo. The officeholder as careerist was not a dishonorable thing in itself, John Andrews had come to feel, but it involved certain dangers he'd rather steer clear of. It called for a certain personality type that simply wasn't him.

No, he'd rather just give the legislative role his best shot for six years and then hand it off to someone else, someone fresh. "Heck," he jokingly told people, "I see an argument for term limits every time I look in the mirror." The fallenness of our human condition was no mere theological abstraction to John. The seduction of power had been all too real to him ever since Watergate. So handing off his seat was not a hard decision. By no means, however, did he want to hand off the president's gavel to the other party.

Though never rigidly partisan, Andrews believed the state was better off in the hands of the party that stressed what government can do *to* you, than under the party that stressed what government can do *for* you. Better off, that is, with Republicans rather than Democrats calling the shots. He'd therefore go all out to retain a GOP majority in the Senate when Coloradans voted in November 2004. Or... nearly all out.

Republicans' most vulnerable seat appeared to be that of Sen. Bruce Cairns in Aurora. The incumbent's purist conservative voting record was a poor fit for the district. If he'd step aside for a more electable candidate, an attractive patronage job likely awaited. It fell to Andrews to sell his friend on making such a sacrifice, but in the upshot John's arm-twisting couldn't overcome Bruce's stubbornness. SD-26 was lost, and with it the Republicans' 18–17 edge.

Preparing to swallow the bitter pill of handing over Senate control to the pugnacious Joan Fitz-Gerald and her Democrats, Andrews ruefully admitted to himself that whatever his political gifts might be, winning by intimidation (think Bob Bullock in Texas) wasn't one of them.

Citizenship Deficit

Losing the state Senate was just one part of a larger unraveling for the Colorado GOP that year. They also lost the state House for the first time since Watergate back in the '70s, and they failed to retain the U.S. Senate seat that Ben Nighthorse Campbell had held since 1993. Beer magnate Pete Coors beat former congressman Bob Schaffer in the Republican primary — Schaffer's failure to regain office after having kept his self-limit promise perhaps validating the expedient decision of Tom Tancredo not to keep his — but Coors then lost to Democrat Ken Salazar in the fall.

It was the first shock wave of a methodically-planned and -executed Democrat takeover in Colorado, later chronicled in Rob Witwer and Adam Schrager's brilliant little book, *The Blueprint.* The lark that John Andrews had enjoyed back in the summer as a delegate to the Republican National Convention in New York City, the first time he or Donna had attended an RNC since Nixon days in 1972, seemed cold comfort now at year-end, albeit President Bush had easily won reelection against John Kerry.

Andrews' seventh decade at the political parade took shape as a season when he would stretch himself in new ways to teach and to motivate for the keeping of the Republic. America, he believed, confronted a deeper problem than the budget deficits and trade deficits, education gaps or defense shortfalls, so much discussed in the media. America faced a citizenship deficit.

Wherever you looked, too many people were content to just roll along in what seemed the nation's endless affluence, heedless of the duty, devotion, discipline, effort, and sacrifice essential to sustaining a free society. By 2008, John's alarm at this worsening trend would find voice in his responsibility book, explicitly titled "a citizen's guide." Already, though, leaving elective office as 2005 came on, he was taking every opportunity to teach — and sometimes preach — about that deficit and its dangers.

He helped lead a weekly seminar on great books and political thought for honor students at the Colorado School of Mines. He wrote a column every week or two for the *Denver Post*, and hosted "Backbone Radio" on 710 KNUS every Sunday evening. And his "Head On" mini-debates continued to air daily on Colorado Public Television. Kid in a candy store.

In addition, everything he had learned as a hands-on legislator, and the far-reaching fellowship of kindred spirits he had formed through State Policy Network, seemed to have found their ideal outlet when he joined the California-based Claremont Institute to do state relations and congressional liaison. Andrews had long admired Claremont's bracing advocacy of constitutional conservatism. His affiliation with them was a three-year feast.

Zest for Combat

He relished the chance to both go deeper than he'd ever personally done with the self-evident truths America was founded on, and to develop practical applications of those truths in politics and policy. Constantly on the road, he became a resource for legislators from Arizona, Oklahoma, and Nebraska, to Kansas, Ohio, and Pennsylvania, to Alabama, Mississippi, and Tennessee. With the institute's president, Brian Kennedy, he was often in Washington, talking national security with allies such as Sen. Jeff Sessions, later to serve as President Trump's attorney general, and FBI agent John Guandolo, a leading expert on the Islamic threat.

The job was like taking a high-level graduate seminar — for pay. He met the venerable Harry V. Jaffa, whose books on Lincoln's statesmanship spoke powerfully to him, and the old man's circle of disciples, "Claremonsters" as they called themselves, such keen minds as Charles Kesler, Tom Krannawitter, Tom West, John Marini, Bill Rood, Chris Flannery, and Edward Erler.

The institute's cast of characters was worthy of a movie script. Ken Masugi and John Eastman had been Justice Clarence Thomas's first tutors in conservative constitutionalism. Michael Anton's seminal essay "The Flight 93 Election" would play a role in Donald Trump's stunning 2016 victory. Eastman would be at Trump's elbow (and pay dearly for it) as a legal advisor when victory slipped away from him in 2020.

And, oh yes, it had been a young Jaffa who shaped Goldwater's galvanizing campaign rhetoric in 1964. Andrews was to feel ever indebted to Matt Dunn, a brainy young dentist who had interned at the Independence Institute, for brokering the Claremont connection. Kathleen Chandler, the best admin he'd ever worked with, ran the Claremont State Relations office in downtown Denver.

During those years, John indulged his zest for political combat by championing a couple of hotly contested ballot issues. A 2005 proposal to ensure that Colorado would no longer be a sanctuary for illegal immigrants, which John co-chaired with former Democratic governor Dick Lamm, was off to a roaring start before getting thrown off the ballot on a legal technicality. A 2006 measure to impose term limits on all state judges, rebuking the judiciary for too much activism and too little accountability, seemed headed for passage in October but was dragged down by a barrage of trial-lawyer money in November.

Was Andrews ahead of his time? At the date of this writing, nearly twenty years on, neither issue has yet been satisfactorily addressed in Colorado.

Fatal drag finally overtook his Claremont project as well. It was the too-familiar tale all over again: the mission-blur that comes with being a larger entity's distant satellite office (viz. Shavano Institute) and the improvisational stumbles that beset any skunk works (viz. TCI News).

Face it, he told himself at last. The 6-Up wasn't selling, and the fizz was going flat. Come the financial crisis of 2008, with fundraising woes for so many nonprofits, John Andrews and Brian Kennedy decided it was time for an amicable parting of the ways.

Going Deeper

Andrews sensed an inflection point. New faces were leading the political parade, or soon would be. Colorado

Democrats had recaptured the governorship when Bill Ritter succeeded Bill Owens in 2007. Bush and Cheney would turn over the White House to either McCain or Obama in 2009. But how much difference would any of it really make? Switching out parties or personalities at the top was merely cosmetic unless Americans could rouse themselves and face up to the citizenship deficit.

The man in the mirror frowned at John, and he flinched. So do something, came the unspoken dare. Okay, but what could one person do, one voice among 300 million? Entering his 65th year, he was now his own boss as he had never been before. Was it finally time to write "that book" (subject and contents unknown) which he'd been promising himself to undertake for years? The book his brother, Jim, had long been patiently goading him to tackle, arguing plausibly enough that short-form political commentary didn't have scope for a message that would endure?

John had to admit it was so. Fluent as it might be, his voluminous output on TV, radio, and newsprint amounted thus far to a whole that was much less than the sum of its parts. Time to buckle down and go deeper. The second half of 2008 thus became game-on for the manuscript that would eventually become *Responsibility Reborn.*

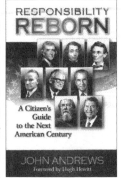

Have book, will flog

The transition from columnist to author proved tougher than he had expected. Knocking out 600 words for the *Denver Post* in two or three hours was easy, whereas developing a thesis across a string of chapters was anything but. In writing long, there was the danger of serving up what Churchill famously called a "themeless pudding." He realized it was going to take near-monastic discipline and the ruthless exclusion of distractions. By way of a cell, he was given the use of a windowless office by Denver businessman Don Siecke, an unselfed benefactor of good causes since John's father's day, forty years earlier.

Element R, the fanciful notion of a responsibility movement rising up from America's grassroots to transcend partisan politics, had recently been floated in the Andrews column a couple of times. John had a hunch there was a book in that, and now set himself to find out. The authorial forced march was on.

His monkish isolation wasn't total, of course. Two moments would remain as landmarks in memory. Sen. John McCain, having bested Mitt Romney for the Republican presidential nomination, stopped in Denver for a fundraiser at the storied Brown Palace Hotel. On being introduced, Andrews told the ex-Navy pilot and heroic former POW how impressed he had been with a talk McCain's father, then commander-in-chief of U.S. forces in the Pacific (CINCPAC), had given at Sub Base Pearl Harbor in 1969.

Eons ago, all that seemed now. Could the Arizona senator beat Barack Obama, and if so, would he do well as president? John Andrews had his doubts on both counts.

Armstrong and Son

The other vivid memory from that period, and much more consequential for John personally, evokes an evening in August 2008 when Wil Armstrong, son of the former senator, was dining with a dozen friends to watch the primary election returns in his bid to succeed the retiring Congressman Tom Tancredo.

Armstrong *fils* ended up losing that race to Secretary of State Mike Coffman—but during dinner Armstrong *pere* expressed delight at learning John was between jobs and writing a book. "When you finish it, join me at CCU and we'll start a policy institute," he boomed down the long table in his inimitable radio baritone.

Bill had taken the presidency of Colorado Christian University a couple of years back, and intended to put it on the map as a lighthouse of conservative thought. John went to bed that night still unsure of how 2008 would play out, for him or for the country, but elated at the new opportunity that it appeared 2009 had in store.

William L. Armstrong, Jr., was Colorado's "Mr. Republican" for a quarter-century beginning in the 1960s. And he was the closest thing John Andrews had to a patron and mentor in spectating at, and sometimes marching in, the endless political parade.

The Nebraska-born broadcaster and businessman was GOP majority leader in the state Senate, then the party's nominee for lieutenant governor, then a congressman for six years, then a U.S. senator for twelve years. Conservative kingmakers courted him to run for president in 1988, but he turned that down and retired from elective office in 1990.

Along the way, he boosted the Independence Institute to some of its early successes, arranged a Reagan advisory appointment for Andrews, and strongly backed John's 1990 gubernatorial bid while other party figures were making themselves scarce. In 1998, Bill Armstrong sided against his own successor, Sen. Hank Brown, to support John Andrews in the Senate vacancy race. He installed his son Wil to manage John's 2000 reelection campaign, lobbied (unsuccessfully) for John to primary Tom Tancredo in 2004 over the term limits issue, and lent his prestige to John's fledgling radio show in 2005.

So there was a certain inevitability in the two men's joining forces in 2009 for what would be Andrews' fifth flyer in leading a policy institute of one kind or another. Lessons learned at Shavano, Independence, Texas, and Claremont would all help shape this newest "tank," the Centennial Institute at Colorado Christian University. "I'm going to keep fooling around with these things until I get it right," he jokingly told friends.

He started at CCU in February 2009. The responsibility book was largely written. Barack Obama, taking office a couple of weeks before, had played with a responsibility theme in his inaugural address, but it was a feint. His stated determination to see America fundamentally transformed must be taken in deadly earnest. John Andrews relished this opportunity to make the opposite case.

There was a sense of déjà vu in coming aboard at Colorado Christian to do battle for the goodness and truth of Western civilization and America's founding principles, fully a generation after having gone to Hillsdale on exactly the same mission. Already in 1981, the little school in Michigan had been a lonely outlier on the left-dominated education landscape.

Now in the dawning Age of Obama the conservative worldview was even more severely marginalized in academe, with yesterday's students having become today's progressive professoriate, and their own children—addled by NEA propaganda in the nihilistic K-12 system— populating the 2009 classroom. When political dabblers oblivious to the ever-intensifying battle of ideas (and Andrews knew plenty of such) idly inquired if his aim was to rebrand CCU as the Hillsdale of the West, essentially an 8-Up gambit to poach a bit of 7-Up's market share, there was asperity in his answer.

Didn't they know how high the stakes were, how late the hour was? The fools. He mostly bit his tongue, though, and contented himself with the jaunty reply: "That's phase one. Phase two is when Hillsdale comes to be seen as but the CCU of the East. And phase three, the endgame, is when we both lead the charge to take back higher ed for God and country. Doubters, watch our dust."

No Fun?

President Armstrong's high purpose and urgency weren't shared by all the university's trustees, administrators, and faculty. But there was a core group of loyalists he could rely on, and his vision made headway. Centennial Institute as a force multiplier for that vision

"That wouldn't be any fun," Bill Armstrong would say impishly

drew energy from the burgeoning Tea Party movement throughout 2009. It was in early 2010 that Andrews was handed a challenge from Armstrong that was to become Centennial's trademark.

The headlines were full of CPAC, the big annual conservative conference in Washington. Why not put on our own big annual conference right here in the Rockies, Bill proposed. Great idea, boss, said John, I'll draw up a plan for summer a year from now.

"Oh, that wouldn't be any fun," countered Armstrong as only he could. "Let's kick it in high gear and pull off the event *this* summer." Andrews gulped, saluted, and raced back to his desk to begin frantic preparations. Thus was born the Western Conservative Summit.

It was a sprint to get that first year's conference programmed, provisioned, and promoted in the few weeks available. But with a valiant team effort drawing on organizers like Joyce Beckett, fundraisers like June Weiss, professors like Greg Schaller, and students like Matt Lenell, they pulled it off. Aiming for attendance around 300, Andrews was pleasantly shocked when 700 turned out.

The speaker lineup featured Michele Bachmann, the fiery Minnesota congresswoman, famed pollster and consultant Dick Morris, and Colorado's own conservative darling, Michelle Malkin. Bill Armstrong's unerring flair for the dramatic prompted inclusion of a 2012 presidential preference straw poll and a parchment of patriotic principles that summiteers were invited to sign, the Lone Tree Declaration.

Morris, though best known for his prior affiliation with President Bill Clinton, had also done campaign work for then senator Bill Armstrong, whom he held in highest esteem. His offline huddles with 2010 congressional hopefuls Cory Gardner and Scott Tipton during the Summit had something to do with both men's eventual upsets of incumbent Democrats that November.

The Western Conservative Summit was off and running for another dozen years of invaluable contributions to CCU's national influence and prestige, with the irrepressible Jeff Hunt eventually taking the reins after John Andrews retired.

Capstone

The political parade in Colorado, meanwhile, at that first midterm election of the Obama years, was taking on a tragicomic cast. Cue the clowns. A wave election across the country, with big losses for the president's party, seemed likely. Colorado Republicans, though, had missed out on the last national wave back in 1994, and John Andrews wondered ominously if 2010 would be another letdown for his side.

Hopes rose when the smell of scandal took Democratic Gov. Bill Ritter out of contention for a second term. Scandal then overtook the presumptive Republican nominee, former congressman Scott McInnis, however, leaving political newcomer Dan Maes as the GOP gubernatorial challenger to face the Democrats' formidable standard-bearer, Denver Mayor John Hickenlooper.

Andrews was sympathetic to the determined, likable Maes, having been in a similar spot himself twenty years before—the dog that caught the car—and he held out stubbornly against Tom Tancredo's third-party candidacy even as most of the Republican establishment lined up with Tancredo and deserted Dan Maes.

When the dust settled on Nov. 3, Democrats had held on to both the governor's chair and Michael Bennet's vulnerable U.S. Senate seat. Republicans did, as mentioned above, flip two U.S. House seats (Gardner and Tipton joining 61 other freshmen to reclaim Congress for the GOP), and they won back the Colorado House, where John's friend Frank McNulty became speaker.

Still it was an ugly year for Colorado Republicans overall. Order, morale, cohesion, and vision in the party of the right have never been the same, down to the time of this writing.

John Andrews would not cease insisting that America's resilient, balanced, and competitive two-party system is the best idea our Founders never had.

Those years at Colorado Christian University were as grand a capstone to his public career as Andrews could possibly have wished for. What work he'd be at, nearing age 70, how long it would occupy him, or when and how it would end, hadn't been planned in the slightest. It was utter serendipity — but a perfect fit.

Bill Armstrong was the kind of leader you'd follow anywhere, a pure delight to work for and work with. Centennial Institute went from strength to strength, each year's Western Conservative Summit gaining in attendance and brightening in reputation.

CCU's newly established political science major — amazingly, there had been none when Armstrong arrived in 2006 — funneled students into Centennial's intern program, dubbed the 1776 Scholars. Young stars such as Brittany Corona, Jonathan Finer, Jamie Erker, and Josh Sherwood were soon making their presence felt. Jeannie Jasper Edwards, buoyant and expert, commandingly took charge of the operational juggling act that Centennial had become.

John Andrews still found time to fiddle around with opinion journalism on KNUS radio, public television, and the *Denver Post*, but he gradually began handing off those slots to a younger generation in the persons of Matt Dunn, Krista Kafer, and Ross Kaminsky. Was he at last growing tired of the sound of his own voice? Increasingly, the unspoken nudge from his brother, Jim, "Long form, Pard, long form," poked at John whenever he sat down to knock out a column. Finally in 2011 he dusted off the *Responsibility Reborn* manuscript.

Overstocked

Agreeably surprised that the book still read pretty well after two years in the drawer, he gave it a final polish, obtained a gracious foreword from radio host (and fellow Nixon man) Hugh Hewitt along with flattering blurbs from Ed Meese, Bill Bennett, and other conservative luminaries, and began looking in earnest for a publisher. This, he learned, required first grinding out a book proposal and hiring an agent. The literary market responded with a vast collective yawn. Reality check: Colorado, where he had been a big fish politically for years, was but a small pond nationally.

Enter Kevin Miller, founding dean of the CCU Business School. He had just done a book with a Denver-based startup called Denali Press, headed by Bob Grizzle and Rex Rolf. Introductions were made, and a deal was reached. Grizzle and Rolf knew what they were about. A handsome volume rolled off the presses, four thousand copies. Promotion kicked off at the 2011 Summit. A couple of local book-signing events helped generate buzz about the man and his message. The flogging process began eating big chunks of John's time.

Denali Press, however, turned out to be woefully undercapitalized. Sustaining the burn rate for national promotion and distribution of both the Miller book and the Andrews book soon proved too much for Grizzle and his investors. The two authors finally had to buy out their broke publisher for pennies on the dollar. Chagrined, John wound up in somewhat the same situation as Thoreau, who boasted sardonically that while his personal library numbered nearly a thousand volumes, most of them were unsold copies of a single book he himself had penned. Ouch.

It was Thoreau's friend Emerson who famously said, "Events are in the saddle and ride mankind." John Andrews, during most of his life as recounted here, had seldom undergone that taken-for-a-ride experience. Usually he was on the initiative, or could at least believe himself to be so. An exception was the wild year of 1982, when he almost lost his marriage and almost forsook Colorado for a move back to his native Michigan. Now came another wild year, 2012, when his health broke.

On what began as an ordinary night in May, driving home to Denver after a speech to the Pueblo Tea Party, stabbing pains wracked his body. Between then and December he would undergo three fairly serious surgeries and yet manage — with invaluable help from Donna and the Centennial Institute staff — to stay on the job with little slackening of pace. At no point was he in fear for his life, but mortality had staked its claim. It was a lesson in trust and gratitude, a gauntlet of uncertainty after which one never again takes life for granted.

John's grandson Ian, soon to be ten, took an interest in that year's Western Conservative Summit as never before. American history and government were beginning to fascinate him. In due time he would find himself enrolled at CCU, studying politics and philosophy.

One night in early fall, Donna and John took Ian to the high school named in memory of her brother, education reformer David D'Evelyn, to see the Republican presidential nominee, Mitt Romney. Andrews had met Rep. Paul Ryan, the former governor's running mate, back in his Claremont days, but he didn't know Romney himself. The Massachusetts Mormon moderate, reinvented for campaign purposes as a "severe conservative," had so far engendered little confidence or enthusiasm on the right. His speech at the D'Evelyn stadium was forgettable.

Andrews wished the GOP would ditch its failed quadrennial formula for anointing White House aspirants, "Next up, your turn." The hereditary approach had bombed with Dole in 1996 and again with McCain in 2008. Too late now for 2012, he thought ruefully, but maybe 2016 would be different. Would it ever.

TABLE: Vital Signs, 2010

	1950	1960	1970	1980	1990	2000	2010	2020
Per Capita GDP (a)	$15,559	$19,614	$25,973	$32,377	$40,361	$49,911	$53,683	$62,333
Inflation	$1.00	$1.23	$1.61	$3.42	$5.43	$7.16	$9.06	$10.75
National Debt (b)	76%	43%	35%	31%	52%	55%	87%	126%
Defense Spending (b)	5.0%	9.0%	8%	5.1%	5.6%	3.1%	4.9%	3.7%
Life Expectancy	68	70	71	74	75	77	78	79
Birth Rate (c)	3.15	3.44	2.38	1.79	1.96	2.01	1.98	1.78
Born to Unwed Mothers	5%	7%	13%	21%	26%	33%	41%	41%
Born Outside USA	7%	5%	4%	6%	8%	11%	13%	14%
High School Completion	34%	40%	48%	63%	70%	83%	86%	90%
Church Attendance (d)	39%	49%	40%	40%	40%	42%	38%	31%

a) Constant 2017 dollars
b) Percent of GDP
c) Per woman lifetime
d) At least weekly

VITAL SIGNS, 2010

The symptoms of national decline don't typically arrive with a thunderclap. They creep over the land like bad air. A decade into the new century, America remained a beacon of hope for the world, as attested by the millions of people thronging to get here from all corners of the earth. Yet the nation's vital signs were worrisome.

Income growth as of 2010 was only a third of what it had been in any decade since 1950. Things felt stagnant. Both parties had lost interest in balancing the budget, and the ever-growing federal government was paid for more and more with borrowed money (table, next-to-last column).

The baby bust persisted, and immigration was surging. The proportion of American children growing up without a stable family structure was approaching one half. On the plus side, high school completion was now about 6 in 7; it had been only 2 in 5 when John was a student in the 1960s. Or was that a plus? The formation kids were acquiring in left-dominated public education might be part of the problem for the country's future, not part of the solution, he reflected grimly.

CHAPTER EIGHT
OBAMA TO TRUMP TO BIDEN

May 2014 – April 2024

Crazy Clairvoyance

SENATOR LELAND VOTES AYE

JOHN ANDREWS

STORIES FROM UNDER THE DOME

The Senator Leland stories posed moral conundrums John
could imagine himself wrestling with
if he had his legislative career to do over

W hat? You're kidding. At a dinner party with a dozen conservative sages on election night 2016, in an utterly accidental flash of brilliance, John Andrews alone predicted Donald Trump's victory over Hillary Clinton. Put it down to dumb luck; even a stopped clock is right twice a day.

Wil Armstrong had convened the gathering in keeping with the time-honored custom of his father, who had died that summer after a long battle with cancer. Terry Considine, Dick Wadhams, Sean Conway, and other political veterans around the table raised their eyebrows and smiled indulgently at John's contrarian flight of fancy. If only.

Then, just a few minutes later, one after another looked with astonishment at their smartphones as major news outlets began reporting the shift of betting odds from Hillary's favor to Trump's. Andrews himself couldn't believe his eyes.

John was now almost a year into his post-CCU career change, having handed the conn to Jeff Hunt and stepped aside from the Centennial Institute at the end of 2015. After favoring Ted Cruz, an old friend and past Summit speaker, during the 2016 presidential primaries, he had become in May the first prominent Colorado Republican to endorse Donald Trump.

It involved eating some crow, since John the previous year had initially dismissed Trump's candidacy as a bad joke and had subsequently, in front of Hugh Hewitt's national radio audience, stopped just short of declaring himself a Never Trumper.

Come 2016, however, with the remarkable surge of Republican voters around Trump's defiant banner in state after state, Andrews decided he should stand with, not against, them. His logic, as he had been saying for years in speeches to whoever would listen, went this way:

Humanity's best earthly hope is America. America's soul is in the truths of her founding documents, the Declaration of Independence and the Constitution. The staunchest defender of those truths is the Republican Party.

That makes our country's Republican Party, imperfect as it is, the most important secular institution on earth; hence worthy of our support for the individual it chooses to contend for the most powerful office on earth.

Andrews, reasoning thus, accordingly backed Trump without reservation or hesitation all the way through the summer and fall campaign with the horrors of October to victory in November and inauguration in January.

Treadmill?

This, the eighth grateful decade of John Andrews' political rambles, had of course officially begun in May 2014. The now familiar, well-oiled countdown to Western Conservative Summit weekend was underway. *How can we top ourselves? How can we outdo last year?* Such had become the perennial question for John and everyone on the team.

For him, at least, it had all begun to feel a bit like a treadmill. *My mama raised an idea broker, not an event promoter,* a little voice grumbled from deep inside.

Previously, they had experimented with a "sister summit" event in Phoenix, with some speakers appearing there live and others linked to Denver via livestream. President Armstrong urged the idea on Andrews as a pilot for what he hoped could become a multi-city extravaganza. It fizzled.

A national young conservatives leadership conference, held at CCU just ahead of the Summit, took hold and thrived, however.

The excitement of what looked to be a good election year for Republicans was in the air at WCS 2014. Congressman Cory Gardner, who had addressed WCS 2010 as a young state legislator on the way up, spoke again this time. Election night would see him upset U.S. Sen. Mark Udall as part of a national GOP sweep. Colorado Republicans also took back the state Senate for the first time in ten years, a source of personal satisfaction to Andrews. The gavel he previously wielded would now pass to his friend Bill Cadman of Colorado Springs.

But the Republican hope of retaking the governorship was not to be. Former congressman Bob Beauprez, the GOP nominee in 2006, led the charge again in 2014, but ultimately couldn't unseat Gov. John Hickenlooper. Hick's political roots in metro Denver tainted him in the hinterlands, though. Leaders in some northern counties became so disgusted with Democrat indifference to rural Colorado that they started a semi-serious secession movement.

One of them, Weld County commissioner Sean Conway, an Armstrong protégé, hired Centennial Institute to do a feasibility study of the idea. It easily qualified as the most quixotic endeavor of John Andrews' thirty-odd years at the helm of five different think tanks.

Such was the endlessly bubbling variety of life in Bill Armstrong's orbit. Next he was dispatching Andrews to Phoenix as producer of a video lecture series bringing the noted theologian Wayne Grudem's book *Politics According to the Bible* to the screen.

Around the edges of it all, John found time to collect a hundred of his best columns and articles into another book of his own, *Backbone Colorado USA*. This one he self-published through Amazon, Denali Press having long since vanished into the maw of capitalist creative destruction.

Good Contagion

Conservatives by the thousand, gathering from forty states for Western Conservative Summit 2015 at the Colorado Convention Center in Denver, struggled to make sense of the recent Supreme Court ruling that found a right to same-sex marriage in the U.S. Constitution. They could find there nothing of the kind. Where was America headed, anyway?

Presiding over the Western Conservative Summit six times, 2010-2015, as attendance climbed into the thousands, John was in his element

John Andrews, convening the opening session, reached back across the millennia all the way to King David and Psalm 144 for part of the answer: "Happy is that people whose God is the Lord." He was determined to be no whit less than unconditionally grateful, hopeful, and joyful in this American moment, let the nine robed justices rule what they may.

Gratitude's good contagion rippled through the packed hall starting right then, and the summiteers were soon up and doing what they had come to do: make a difference for freedom.

For Andrews, this was to be his sixth and last time chairing the Summit. Reflecting and praying with Donna and their children over the past few weeks, he had clearly seen it was time to turn the page. Replacing himself wouldn't be easy, though, John soon realized. The high-pressure juggling act he had created at the Centennial Institute wasn't something that just anyone would want to take on.

Bob Schaffer and Bob Beauprez, two former congressmen who were close to Bill Armstrong, politely took a pass. So did Gino Geraci, a popular local pastor turned broadcaster. The role demanded a young gun, on fire with energy and zeal. Colorado's own Jeff Hunt, who had been helping Andrews with media and messaging, emerged as the perfect fit. They set to work on a handoff in the autumn months of 2015.

The idea of "retiring" hadn't been in John's mind at all when tendering his resignation in late summer, but that was the way Armstrong spun it in announcing the move, so that became the official version. For John, it was mainly a case of burnout, mental exhaustion with the Sisyphean routine of fundraising and speaker bookings, climaxing in the compelling need for a change.

Six or seven or eight years in any one job seemed to have become the pattern for him, for some reason. His CCU tenure would top out at seven as 2016 began. Politics, education, media, and ministry, the career mix that had evolved for him over almost half a century since starting at the White House in 1970, evidently required some abrupt stirring of the pot every few years in order to coax out of John the best he had to give.

Now, just 71, brimming with energy and chafing with new ideas to expend it on, he saw himself not as a retiree but as a freelance thinker and patriot, a role he had played more than once before. Always in the past, though, it had been temporary, transitional. This time it looked to be for the duration.

There was so much writing to be done, and now at last, plenty of time to do it in. Out came *Downstream: An American Album,* essays co-authored with his younger brother, Jim. And

Mort: A Memoir, the story of his wife's family, the D'Evelyns of California. And "Jesus in Pursuit," a monograph that eventually became the nucleus of his spiritual autobiography, *Discovering a Larger God.* And the George Leland political stories, one after another, eight of them in all, finally collected in book form as *Senator Leland Votes Aye.*

He joined several boards, from that of the Presbyterian church where he'd long been a member, to that of Christ's Body Ministries, a shelter in downtown Denver, to that of the Fellowship of Former Christian Scientists, a resource for individuals who were (as he was himself) escapees from false theology and latecomers to biblical faith.

The great issue that now troubled him most was the relentless, insidious Islamic drive for global dominance. In the dozen or so years since bin Laden's September 11 attacks on the U.S. homeland, mass terrorism had been pretty well suppressed, but the underlying menace of jihad and Sharia law continued unchecked, as John Andrews saw it.

He signed on as a program officer with two of the most effective counter-jihad crusaders out there, Frank Gaffney of the Center for Security Policy and John Guandolo of Understanding the Threat. He set up a nonprofit, nonpartisan educational foundation called Americans for America that contracted with Guandolo's group for grassroots organizing work across the country: Texas, Tennessee, Virginia, Kansas, Oklahoma, Minnesota, California.

He joined the U.S. delegation at an all-European conference on the issue in Warsaw in 2017. He aroused a gratifying howl of outrage by warning against the poisonous ideas of Mohammed and Marx when he was invited back to address the Western Conservative Summit in 2019.

No Gained Causes

Yet the political parade as such no longer seemed to fascinate and divert him as it had once done, Andrews was surprised to find. Was it partly just a result of having watched from the front row so avidly for so long? Ecclesiastes was right, he saw: there's not a lot that's new under the sun. Nor do the hardest-fought contests and the loudest-shouted slogans end up effecting that much real change. There are no lost causes because there are finally no *gained* causes, as T.S. Eliot remarked.

More and more, John's mind went back to the hole that's *not* left when you pull your fist out of a bucket of water. Less and less could he have named, if his life depended on it, the leaders of the state Senate and House — the names that had seemed to him so illustrious, so immortal, when his own was among them, not so many years ago.

He clung, though, to his oft-expressed conviction that the battle is its own reward. To serve honorably, stand strong, and keep faith counts for something, he insisted; counts for much. If life, public life included, is at last no more than a holding action against entropy, so be it. Far better to be counted among those who held, than among those who found an excuse not to.

Where had the years gone? One day it struck him that when his eighth grateful decade wrapped up in May 2024, he would be as distant in time from the day of his birth in May 1944 as had been his parents then — the young bride Marianne, the young submariner John — from the dark days of America's civil war in May 1864. Astonishing.

What had seemed to little John, getting his first taste of history and politics from his mother's brother, state

Sen. Edward Hutchinson, the vast expanse of time from Lincoln to FDR, was in fact no greater than the relative blink of an eye from Truman to Biden that state Sen. John Andrews had now lived through, eighty grateful years. Perspective is everything.

The olden days, Grandfather's times, have always seemed mythic and remote in the eyes of the younger generation looking back. "There were giants in the earth in those days," we've always tended to think (Gen. 6:4). Whereas in reality each generation just muddles through and does its best. Epochs and dates aside, a single human lifetime can be as consequential or inconsequential as one makes it. And the cup that runneth over with gratitude is free to all who thirst.

Twenty twenty came, the year of plague and riots. The presidency changed hands, albeit Trump showed ill grace with his grudging departure. Twenty twenty-two came, the year of the red wave that wasn't. Republicans took back the U.S. House, albeit Democrats in Colorado entrenched themselves deeper than ever. John Andrews could hardly remember a time when the parade seemed more lackluster.

Yet the holding action by conservatives, seen across the longer span of decades, hadn't gone all that badly, he felt. If his beloved Colorado wasn't as conservative as, say, Texas, neither was she as liberal as California. Not yet anyway. If the country itself wasn't as conservative as, say, Nixon might have wished, neither was she as liberal as Johnson stubbornly intended.

What great nation on the world stage, for that matter, as 2024 ripened, stood anywhere near as tall as America in exemplifying liberty and limited government, opportunity and affluence, generosity and compassion, justice and mercy? To be alive at such a time and place, amid such a cloud of witnesses: what a glory!

Declaration

For an 80th birthday present, therefore, Andrews decided to give himself — or actually, his descendants — this little book as a Declaration of Gratitude. He would name the names that needed thanking, tell the stories that needed remembering, and spin the yarns that needed spinning. Get it all on record before memory faded and the curtain came down.

So: an autobiography? Not exactly. He wouldn't try for a rounded self-portrait, the man in full. Just to reflect on the civic, political, public dimension of his life would be challenge enough. And he'd write in the third person, as if all these things had happened to someone else — waiving any notion that the center of the 1944–2024 panorama had been *him*, for heaven's sake.

A decidedly off-center viewpoint, that's what he'd take from beginning to end. And in fact, let's see, harking back to some American lit class he'd taken in college, who was it who had narrated his own life in the third person? Henry Adams, that was it, the quintessential cosmopolitan Bostonian, grandson and great-grandson of presidents.

John got hold of an audiobook edition of *The Education of Henry Adams* and really liked it. (Much of his reading was now done that way, via the spoken word; doctors had ordered lots of daily exercise to combat what might be Parkinson's disease.)

Adams' tone of dry detachment proved to be just what Andrews was looking for. To write with candor and color, yet never take oneself a hundred percent seriously: this seemed the recipe for a narrative that wouldn't cloy. Whether it has succeeded here, the reader can judge.

This account that John Andrews now began to see as his Declaration of Gratitude was necessarily also, he realized, a declaration of dependence. Americans must not confuse their political independence from external rulers, grounded in eternal self-evident truths, with their inescapable, beneficial mutual dependence on each other in the moral, cultural, social, and economic dimension.

If a long life had taught him anything, it was that an atomized world of self-centered absolutist individualism was not a world he'd want to live in. Gratitude implies fellowship. Gratitude means not only thankfulness *for* the good things in our experience, but also thankfulness *to* the giver and source of those good things.

"There is a God, and I'm not him." This simple realization is the starting point of all sound theology and anthropology, indeed of all practical wisdom and sane common sense. If you see a turtle on a fencepost, it's been said, you know he didn't get there by himself. The humility and realism to recognize our dependent condition, our "turtleness," is a great asset for living well. The wonderment and questing spirit that aspires to know Whose hand elevated us is a greater asset still.

The springtime of 2024, the last few weeks before John Andrews' eighth grateful decade would officially close on May 1st, his birthday, brought one milestone after another prompting him to take stock, take the long view. Fifty years of life together in the Colorado home he liked to call Marcus Bend in honor of his grandfather. Fifty-seven years of his marriage with Donna, and the same 57 years since his commissioning as a naval officer.

Thirty-four years since he had plunged into a no-hope race for governor. Passion Week and Easter, of little importance to him when following Mrs. Eddy and Christian Science up until the 1990s, but all-important now that he followed Jesus.

Sacred Season

It became a sacred season of gratitude for him. He thanked God for the blessing of having been born in the land of the free, for his early grounding in the Bible, for his family roots in Michigan and Missouri and his mountain summers in Colorado, for his education at Principia, for the noble soul that was his brother and the indomitable women who were his two sisters, for joining his life with Donna's and entrusting them with Tina, Jen, Daniel, and Ian, dearer to him than life itself.

He thanked God for meaningful work and the opportunity to contribute — would that he had contributed more, alas — in the Navy, at the White House, at Adventure Unlimited, at Hillsdale, at Independence Institute, in Texas, in cable news, at Greater Europe, at Claremont, and at Centennial Institute.

He thanked God for those few grand occasions when good fortune — no, divine purpose, inscrutable though it might have been — placed him not just at but *in* the crazy political parade: the heady times of speechwriting for President Nixon, and of taking on Governor Romer, and of championing the Constitution as a state senator. Would that he had known then, in those palmy days so long ago, some of what he knew now.

Look, coming into sight now, behind the brass band, isn't that Johnnie A? See him, wearing the MAGA hat, just behind the tubas and trombones? But why is he totally out of step? Oops, I get it now. All the other marchers, they're the ones out of step.

Sorry, where was I? A sacred season of gratitude, that's right. Rounding out his eight grateful decades in those lovely spring weeks of 2024, John Andrews above all thanked God for simply being God, the Lord of History and the High King of Heaven. He thanked God for making us in his image, for redeeming us through the Cross, and for endowing us with the capacity for self-government under his guiding hand.

Alexander Hamilton said in *Federalist No. 1* that the American founding posed the question of whether mankind can achieve good government by "reflection and choice" rather than by "accident and force." Andrews thanked God that so far at least, almost 250 years on, the question seemed to have been answered in the affirmative. But he offered a silent prayer for whatever may come next, remembering that there are no gained causes.

For himself and for his loved ones, though, he felt certain that the best was yet to be. Earth's political parade in all its proud pomp and gaudy glamor was but the palest foreshadowing of the heavenly celebration and reunion set to welcome the sons and daughters of the King at the last day.

There were mornings when John, coping with creaky joints and foggy faculties, felt as if his own last day might not be that far distant now. At other times, most of the time in fact, he was full of life and afire with anticipation for what the future might hold. If President Biden and former President Trump, both close to him in age, could keep answering the bell every morning, so could he.

Andrews had never met either man, but he had gotten to Washington three years ahead of Biden back in the 1970s and had kept a wary eye on the hardballer ever since—and with Donna he had been in the front row at a Trump campaign event in Denver in 2016.

Only once before in American history, with the Cleveland-Harrison contest of 1892, had an incumbent president faced his predecessor in an electoral rematch. This was going to be a showdown for the ages, John Andrews told himself. He'd probably not see anything like this again if he lived to be a hundred.

VITAL SIGNS, 2020

The good news: Americans in 2020 were living more than a decade longer than they had in 1950, and their real income had quadrupled over those 70 years (table, right column).

The bad news: not even in 1944, when John Andrews was born, with the nation fighting for its life in World War II, had government debt exceeded 112 percent of GDP. It was now at 126 percent, and hadn't appreciably decreased by 2024 when this book went to press. No one is so foolish as to eat their seed corn, he told himself with a shudder. *Or are they?*

His table of vital signs, all eight decades now accounted for, wasn't a rosy picture overall. The demographic indicators, all moving negatively since the 1970s, continued to worsen. And religious observance, generally steadily throughout the late 20th century, had fallen by about one fourth in these early years of the 21st century.

Was it any wonder that appeals to restore America's greatness were showing so much political potency?

	1950	1960	1970	1980	1990	2000	2010	2020
Per Capita GDP (a)	$15,559	$19,614	$25,973	$32,377	$40,361	$49,911	$53,683	$62,333
Inflation	$1.00	$1.23	$1.61	$3.42	$5.43	$7.16	$9.06	$10.75
National Debt (b)	76%	43%	35%	31%	52%	55%	87%	126%
Defense Spending (b)	5.0%	9.0%	8%	5.1%	5.6%	3.1%	4.9%	3.7%
Life Expectancy	68	70	71	74	75	77	78	79
Birth Rate (c)	3.15	3.44	2.38	1.79	1.96	2.01	1.98	1.78
Born to Unwed Mothers	5%	7%	13%	21%	26%	33%	41%	41%
Born Outside USA	7%	5%	4%	6%	8%	11%	13%	14%
High School Completion	34%	40%	48%	63%	70%	83%	86%	90%
Church Attendance (d)	39%	49%	40%	40%	40%	42%	38%	31%

a) Constant 2017 dollars
b) Percent of GDP
c) Per woman lifetime
d) At least weekly

EPILOGUE
Sky Valley Ranch
May 2044

A Century of Gratitude

Ian Andrews, age 17, with his grandfather at Sky Valley Ranch in 2020

This would have been John Andrews' one-hundredth birthday. He wasn't able to be present in person, but at his behest several dozen friends and family were gathered on the lawn of an imposing log lodge at Sky Valley Ranch near Buena Vista, Colorado.

The weather at 8500 feet elevation in the shadow of the Continental Divide could be chancy at this time of year, but they were favored with a sparkling spring morning on the first day of May 2044 for their celebration of the late senator's long and remarkable life.

Sky Valley was the summer camp his father and mother had established way back in the 1950s, still going strong after lo these many seasons. It had been the dearest place on earth to John, the place where he had first met Donna, and he had specified it as the setting for the commemoration now about to take place.

As far back as 2024, having reached the biblical fourscore years and penned a little book gratefully chronicling those eight decades, John had caught himself starting to "think old" and had resolved, with the wife of his youth, for them to desist from all such thinking henceforth. They undertook instead to live in the now, take each day as it came—and what a difference that made!

They had promised each other a dance at their grandson's wedding, and that happy day came, soon followed by great-grandchildren. They had prayed for a cooling of tempers and a renewal of comity and a rededication of American politics to the permanent things, and rejoiced to see all of that beginning to occur in the 2030s. John wrote several more books, trotted a few more times in the Bolder Boulder 10k, even forged his way up one last 14er at age 86.

As the years mounted, somewhat to their surprise, into another grateful decade and then another, he joked that they might as well hang on all the way to a hundred years, "give or take a hundred days" — and so it proved to be. When they died within a few hours of each other on April 16th, their wedding anniversary, John's centenary in May and Donna's in July were both in arm's reach.

Funerals for each were duly conducted at their church in Denver, and they were laid to rest at the nearby Fort Logan National Cemetery. Now they were back — in spirit anyway — in John's beloved high country for this day of fond remembrance.

Book, Sword, Cross

The program started with a solo guitarist singing a wistful, lilting ballad about Don Quixote. As he finished amid soft applause, as at a golf match, a tall, handsome man in his forties, his striking red hair and beard flecked with gray, stood and walked to the podium, microphone in hand.

He glanced out at the rugged, snow-clad peak of Mount Princeton several miles south, then nodded gravely to his wife and children, seated at front row left, and to his parents and aunts and uncles at front row right. The two chairs at front row center sat empty in tribute to his grandmother and grandfather. On one was placed a huge bouquet of roses; on the other, a tricorn-folded flag and Senate gavel.

"Good morning and welcome," the tall man said. "I'm Ian Andrews, the son of Daniel and Stephanie, grandson of John and Donna. Being as I'm fairly at home in the pulpit, Papa asked me to serve as the host today.

"He has this whole thing scripted, it won't surprise you to hear. Because when didn't he?" (Laughter, more applause.) "Once a speechwriter, always a speechwriter, I guess. Any meeting that JKA Jr. walked into, he was probably going to end up chairing." (More laughter.)

"We should thank Aaron Cross again for that fine old Gordon Lightfoot song, so fitting to my Papa's lifelong idealism." (Scattered golf claps.) "John told me that was the unofficial theme song for his 1990 governor's race, the doomed crusade as he laughingly called it. Look at the lyrics again later. They picture the battered book, the rusty sword, above all the tarnished cross — and those were the tools of his trade.

"His trade, of course, was politics, always politics, right there in the front row. But that wasn't all. There was also education, also media, also ministry. He wove them together, all four of them, in his own special way. He was always reminding us, in fact, not to make too much of politics, as if government were the main thing. It's not!

"'*How small, of all that human hearts endure, that part which laws or kings can cause or cure.*' Papa loved those lines from Dr. Samuel Johnson, one of his literary heroes. And what a classically conservative insight. He especially wanted me to convey it to you today. Listen to hearts. Minister to hearts. Hearts matter most.

"So I hope the memories that all of you will share when we open the floor a few minutes from now will range across the whole span of who John Andrews was and all the things he was passionate about.

"To get us started, and remembering that we are still on the JKA Jr. script here — *no going off script!* — we'll hear from my father about the adventurer that John was, from my Aunt Jen about the competitor John was, and then—wait for it—from my Aunt Tina about the clown John sometimes was.

"So, TT and JJ, do tell. Who were No. 99 and No. 44? Who was Chuckles? But, Dad, you're first. What really went down on the infamous Mosquito Island?"

As Daniel stepped forward and took the mic from Ian, a breeze rustled the grove of pines uphill to the left, and horses whinnied in a nearby pasture. Then a hush fell. In that moment of sun-drenched mountain stillness, every member of the gathered Andrews family was reliving in their mind's eye this or that vivid scene of the ghost parade from decades past.

Ten of them, in fact, grateful decades all, gifts from a gracious God to these dear children of his, Johnnie A and Donna Marie.